of the principles he evolves to the broad problem of musical criticism. He demonstrates how the meaning of music is relevant and necessary to a true evaluation or criticism of music. On the basis of these theories and conclusions, he proposes and outlines a new system of musical criticism, one which he hopes will provide a sounder basis than that which is based solely on analysis of musical structure.

The book will be of interest to musicians, music lovers, music critics, aestheticians, and others interested not only in music itself but in the philosophical and psychological questions which it raises.

Donald N. Ferguson is a professor emeritus of music at the University of Minnesota and former head of the department of music at Macalester College. He is the author of several other books, including *Masterworks of the Orchestral Repertoire: A Guide for Listeners* (see back of jacket) and for many years has been the program annotator for the Minneapolis Symphony Orchestra.

MUSIC AS METAPHOR

Donald N. Ferguson

MUSIC AS METAPHOR

The Elements of Expression

UNIVERSITY OF MINNESOTA PRESS

Minneapolis

For Arline

Preface

THIS book is a drastic revision of the verbal substance, but hardly at all of the general thesis, of a study put forth in mimeograph some twenty years ago under the title, "On the Elements of Expression in Music." The author's effort was then, and is still, to account in a rational manner for certain values which the great majority of music lovers find in their art, and which they confidently accept as "expressive" — as utterances, portrayals, intimations, or whatever — relative to non-musical experience. To define these values — to describe both the manner in which the musical substance functions for expression and also the product of that functioning — is the main purpose of our effort; but to establish expression as a value not to be ignored in the process of criticism is also its objective.

The bearing of expression on the problem of criticism will be noted, here and there, as occasion arises. But since expressiveness in all art, but especially in music, is now-a-days largely minimized, and in some quarters dismissed as non-existent, we have attempted to set forth, in our preliminary chapter, first the objective of criticism when expression is admitted as one of its essential areas, and then the nature of the problem of expression as a contribution to the whole area of criticism.

In the perspective of the naive music lover, who has no doubt as to the meaning of music for himself, our effort to describe the expressive value of music may well seem a superfluous demonstration of the obvious. In the perspective of the student whose deep concern with the techniques of structure and composition has convinced him that structure and expression are one, our effort may seem presumptuous in the extreme — an attempt to analyze and demonstrate a non-existent function. For expressiveness inevitably implies reference to non-musical experience; music, seen as structure only, bears no such reference; and if these are the actual premises the conclusion is ineluctable that musical expression does not exist. Invisibility, however — especially to myopic vision — is a precarious proof of non-existence.

The function of structure as performed by the operation of cohesive musical elements has been theoretically analyzed and demonstrated in a manner probably as far in accord with scientific method as is possible. (The cohesive forces resident in the scale or in harmony cannot be finally explained by physics, nor are the percepts they evoke clearly traceable psychologically; yet a brave approach to scientific — or at least objective — accuracy has been made by the analysts.) But science will also recognize that the performance of a given function need not necessarily exhaust either all the forces resident in the elements involved, or the possibilities of combining those elements for the performance of quite another than the given function. A new perspective will indeed be required to discover, and a new analysis to demonstrate, this new function. But to deny such a possibility *a priori* is itself an offense against the scientific method in whose name the denial is asserted.

This book attempts such an analysis. Our argument is indeed less "scientific" than rational. Like those who have explored the substance of music to find the elements of structure, we have sought in that same substance for the elements of expression. We have identified them, hypothetically, and have subjected our hypothesis to rather extended experimental tests. The reader will determine for himself how far our hypothesis is supported by the facts. But while the involved facts, in our inquiry, will assume a new aspect, those facts — not merely to the student of music but to the generality of its lovers — are familiar, evident, and indubitable. (If this were not so, music would have no public — and no history.) Also, our hypothesis, whether drawing from musical theory or psychology, proposes nothing really new or obscure, because the aroused awareness of meaning in music — which is a fact of expression — is itself neither new nor obscure. Its *method* does appear enigmatical; so, in the last analysis, is the method of any achieved expression; but as an awareness it is as readily aroused in the untutored mind as in the sophisticated. (In the tutored mind it is often sadly obscured by sophistication.)

Since the facts underlying our hypothesis are familiar, the reader will not be constantly referred to authority, scientific or philosophical (our argument dares to touch the hem of philosophy) for confirmation of our statements. Although our thesis appears to us amply supported by such

viii

authority, it has been compiled, not from such derivative sources, but from musical experience — from perceptions and convictions engendered by the impact of music, chiefly upon the author's mind, but also upon the minds of many students, composers, performers, and amateurs of music with whom, in a long professional activity, he has had the good fortune to deal.

To some of these, it is true, music remained a fascinating object merely — the decoration (and for the fortunate possessor the outward sign) of a privileged existence. To many of them — the more percipient — it proved an extraordinarily vivid counterpart — indeed, a metaphor — for their awareness, not of the things but of the significance of experience.

The significance of experience, as judged by both intelligence and imagination, is our commonest measure of that reality which we feel rather than actually perceive as somehow present behind the bare actualities of daily existence. Great music glimpses that reality. Thus, for the presumptuous effort here set forth I have dared to choose a presumptuous title. For I know nothing more real than my own being, nor illumination of it more metaphoric than that offered by music.

Contents

PROLOGUE

Flower in the crannied wall,
I pluck you out of the crannies: —
Hold you here, root and all, in my hand,
Little flower — but if I could understand
What you are, root and all, and all in all,
I should know what God and man is.

❧ *I* ❧

The Problems of Criticism and Expression

THE main purpose of this book is to offer a rational account of the structural basis and the functional process of musical expression. It will explore, that is, the substance of music as related to vital rather than to purely aesthetic experience. We shall find that the musical illumination of experience may attain to the vividness of metaphor — that music may appear to the sentient listener as the very stuff, not of experience as it is factually seen and intellectually known, but of experience as it lives, largely as an emotional response to factual encounter, in our minds. To explore this emotional consciousness and to find its metaphoric equivalent in the substance of music is indeed a portentous problem.

But to attack the portentous problem of musical expression is to attack also the still larger problem of musical criticism. For criticism, in both its literal and its practical sense, is valuation; and if music, along with its purely artistic appeal, is capable also of intelligible reference to other than purely artistic experience — which is to say, of expression — sound criticism must somehow evaluate this reference. Before attacking the problem of expression itself, we shall therefore summarize that expanded view of the critical effort which must result when the contributions of expression to the whole sum of musical value are acknowledged.

The primary value of music, felt at its first impact on the ear, is sensuous and wholly non-referential — a value clearly akin to that of taste which, whether the discrimination is of the tongue or the mind, the most indisputable authority in the world (a Latin proverb) tells us is not to be disputed. That critical judgment probably holds because taste, even in those manifestations of it which are mental rather than merely gustatory, still involves the immediate attraction or repulsion of a sensory impression; and the value of a sensory impression is hardly a matter for debate.

3

The common enjoyment of a sensory experience does establish, however, a kind of communion among the participants; and community of experience, established, is itself a kind of communication. If, then, along with this sensory offering, reference to other than purely sensuous experience should be included, ideas — the product of experience impinging upon minds — may be generated. And ideas, which are the summaries and interpretations of experience, can be valued.

This is perhaps an over-laborious way of saying that music may possibly evoke ideas relative not merely to the sensuous and structural substance of music itself, but relative also to important aspects of non-musical experience. Verbal definition of the ideas thus evoked by music is all but impossible. Yet the sense of communication music evokes is often as vivid as that achieved by words. The hearer, however, although aware of some sort of communication, is chiefly concerned with the whole pleasurable impact of the musical performance, and will ordinarily accept this "meaning" without inquiry as to the means or the process of its communication, and with more interest in its immediate stimulation than in its relevance to experience. That is, he is not a critic.

If he attempts that role, he finds critical inquiry into the source and the process of such communication difficult to begin and disconcerting to pursue. For he finds that the image of experience evoked in his own mind by a piece of music fails to correspond with that envisioned by another hearer; nothing in the musical substance portrayed or represented any factual detail of the experience he "saw"; the stimulus that excited him was indubitably a musical form; the very substance of music, and still more its organization into a form, is exciting; and if this was his only stimulus, and this his only excitement, the notion that music really expresses any other idea than that of form — or indeed that it *expresses* any idea at all, since the image of form was directly presented, not expressed — seems quite disproved.

Yet if he abandons his role of critic and reverts to his first impression, he is unconvinced. For there *was* an image, however indefinable, of experience. That image, his brief effort at criticism has shown him — through its failure to exorcise the apparition — must be pondered. And, as he ponders, questions begin to arise — questions as disconcerting to himself as critic as were his critical questions to himself as naive listener.

For the testimony of other hearers that music also evoked images for them — images like his own in general, if not in detail — is uncontroverted by the evidence of difference between their images and his own. Some of them, indeed, are all but identical. For no more in music than in any other language is the call to battle the call of the lover to his mate. There is, again, a great body of music associated with religion, some of which bears indubitable relation to religious experience while some of it does not. How, on a basis of form disassociated from experience, is this question of appropriateness to be answered? If it cannot be so answered, must it not follow that the appropriateness is really intrinsic? Granted that both the religious attitude and the response to musical form are in no small part products of convention and habit, does it follow that the association between them is wholly mechanical? And if it is intrinsic, is not a primary fact of expressiveness already established, however obscure the thought expressed or the process of expression?

It is wholly unimaginable that the huge musical public whose growth the history of music chronicles could ever have been assembled solely through the admiration for an art which, however fascinating as art, bore no reference whatever to the experiences that drive men to fight and love and worship. The sensuous appeal of music, however, is high, and the possible varieties of its organization into forms are almost unlimited. Observed, then, as structure merely, the musical organism is much more than a static object. It *is* an organism. Its parts function, and those functions, all correlated and visibly concrescent toward the image of form, yield an object worthy of intense study.

Its field of reference, however, compared to the limitless field of experience, is narrow. With that wider field, the other arts have unimpeded contact. Criticism of those arts, envisaging that contact, reveals that high rewards may accrue to study which thus embraces the experiential reference as well as the immediate and intrinsic interest of the art-work as a formed object. It is thus at least rational to inquire whether the field of musical criticism may be similarly extended.

But no more with music than with any other more representative art can that inquiry be fruitfully pursued by minuter examination of the art-work as a self-contained object. Another process of study will have to be devised, and another scale of values erected — a scale which envisages more than the technical apparatus of structure. Such a scale appears to be succinctly set up in the first sentence of Bacon's essay, *Of Studies*: "Studies serve for delight, for ornament, and for ability."

Delight, indisputably, is an immediate offering of music. Ornament, in

5

Bacon's sense, is of course not the familiar contributor to musical delight, but the product of a thousand subtle contributions to what may perhaps be called refinement. This end music may also serve. But ability — obviously the highest in Bacon's ascending order of values — which at first appears as worldly accomplishment, turns out to be the equivalent, or at least the product, of human understanding; and how music can serve this end is a more difficult question.

That kind of contemplation which results in human understanding may indeed include, in considerable volume, those things which serve for delight and ornament. Neither is their boundary, toward the side of understanding, at all clearly definable. But understanding comprises more than refinement. It embraces a great complex of awarenesses, for which our most adequate verbal symbol is "experience."

The other arts have always unblushingly drawn their subject-matter from discernible facts of experience. Their method is thus often clearly aimed at the purpose we are now thinking of. It is true that so-called "representative" artists often mistake factual representation for that deeper illumination of experience which is the high function of art; but this is the fault, not of their method, but of their imagination. At any rate the arts — rather for their illumination of experience than for their offering of delight and ornament — have been cherished throughout human history above all the other creations of men. Thus, if music's offering comprises no more than delight and ornament, its claim to sisterhood with the other arts must be considerably weakened.

A counter-claim may of course be urged. It is often contended that music, because of its incapacity for portraying those facts of experience with which the other arts deal, is thereby not only released from the irksome necessity of somehow exalting fact into art, but is also, through that very release, itself exalted above the other arts. In this claim, however, there is more of vanity than of logic. No more than music do the other arts exalt fact into art, nor is it their object to illuminate fact. They illuminate experience, which is a distillation of the meaning resident in fact.

Meaning, thus distilled — whether we grasp it through art or science or plain common sense — offers the most dependable discrimination we possess between the true and the false — the real and the unreal. (Ultimate reality appears to be unknowable, even in the field of science.) Our judgment of reality — involving along with the perception of fact the intuitions and the inherent prejudices and preferences of the perceiving mind itself (which cannot be weighed or measured) — thus takes the form of conviction, rather than of absolute certainty. (The Delphic motto, *Know thyself*, originated in a most percipient distillation of experience.) Every individual must therefore extract for himself that distillation which turns fact into experience. All the arts strive to evoke in the beholder's mind an image, not of fact as it is, but of experience *as it is lived*. Music, if it is to achieve the same end, must evoke in the listener a conviction of reality. But experience can be distilled from nothing else than fact, and music, striving to serve for ability, can no more escape dependence on this ultimate basis than can the other arts.

All art is thus an abstraction. Viewed as the unique embodiment of a distillation of fact into experience, it will appear as an abstraction *drawn out of* experience. In this view it may well serve for ability where ability is defined as human understanding. The profounder the experience — judged by those standards of significance which intelligence can erect, and of course assuming that the artist's distillation (or abstraction) is adequate — the more significant the art-work.

Yet the facts contributory to experience are innumerable. Thus the musician's creation — his objectively viewed musical form, created out of sensuously appealing substance and organized so as to impart to that substance the intellectual delight of organization — is itself a distillation of experience; for sensuous stuff is a material, and organization an intellectual, object of experience. A competently contrived musical form must thus be recognized as having not merely the external surface but something of the inner reality of art. But such a form, if it makes no discernible reference to the larger world of experience, and if judged by the standards which that larger world applies, will appear as an abstraction made by *drawing away from* that larger world into the world of art itself.

This, the delectable region of the ivory towers, is not really a separate world. It is only an enclave — one, however, into which citizens of the larger world at first enter with diffidence. For the things displayed there are mostly fragile objects, too delicate for every-day use, yet greatly desirable for their exquisiteness, or their grotesqueness, or for any other quality between those two extremes. Frequent visits to this enclave, however, engender the conviction that no other than these objective values need be assessed. The workers therein are even more positive. Thus, appreciation of their work (appreciation is a rather timid term, often implying conventional response to supposedly authoritative critical evaluation) will appear both to the patron and the artist himself as complete when all the values of substance and organization have been neatly appraised.

An ultimate product of practiced appreciation, often unconsciously formed, is taste — a discrimination more positive when formed within the enclave, where substance and structure alone are the bases of judgment, than in the larger world, where obscurer values of experience must also be considered. The differentia of taste, whether pondered or unconsciously assimilated, when fused and exhibited in a finished art work, yield a general concept of style. Style, accordingly, becomes one of the final criteria for criticism.

Patently, a sensitive awareness of style must comprise an infinity of contributory details. So long as substance and organization remain the only admitted factors of the art work, these details remain pretty clearly definable, and style itself, which may now be learnedly discussed in terms of these definitions, will appear as a comfortably objective fact. But when meaning beyond the implication of substance and structure demands to be considered, these details become subordinate. They will be found to have been chosen, no longer for their intrinsic interest but for their appropriateness to an image of experience as it is lived — no longer the substance of a diaphanous apparition made by drawing away from reality, but contributions to a more comprehensive vision, drawn out of reality itself.

Style, therefore, cannot be adequately defined in terms of structural devices. In spite of the efforts of the rhetoricians, musical or linguistic, to reduce it to those terms, its truest definition is still that of Buffon: *Le style, c'est l'homme même* — the style is the very man — the man in whom experience lives and who makes it live in us.

Music, surely, if it can portray experience as it lives in men, may serve for ability. Criticism, surely, if its problem is a just evaluation of music, may not ignore its expressive achievement. And the problem of expression, our chief concern, we must now attack.

Not in the belief that difficulties may be avoided, but in the hope that they may be lightened, I shall attempt, before entering upon our more precise study, a sort of orientation within the tangled intellectual jungle to be explored. That jungle is the vexed problem of musical expression. To put the problem in focus, I shall ask the reader to share with me the memory of a certain musical experience and to examine in that experience

8

some implications which are vital to our problem. For however remote the questions that must ultimately arise, they all have their origin in some such musical experience as this.

One Saturday evening, during my student days, I was one of many hundreds of listeners who had crowded into the Queen's Hall to hear the rather popular program which Sir Henry Wood had arranged for a Promenade Concert. Having been for long a nightly attendant — except on Saturdays — at that series of concerts, I could see that this audience of unfamiliar faces was drawn from a stratum of music lovers whose interest habitually lay somewhat below the symphonic level. Most of the musical fare had been provided for their taste; but among the somewhat flimsy and threadbare pieces appeared the Violin Concerto in E by Sebastian Bach.

Being myself in a relatively early stage of musical learning, and thus having learned that Bach's music was to be appreciated only by the learned, I expected this work to make but little impression on such an audience. But my sophomoric judgment was quite mistaken. The first movement was received with signs of high approval (even the enlightened, in those days, applauded after every movement of a piece); but after the slow movement — played as I have never heard it before or since — there was an incredibly long interval of absolute silence: of that dumbfounded silence in which men contemplate a revelation. Of course, after we had again descended to ordinary levels of perception, we expressed our thanks for the musical offering in the most convincing roar of applause I can remember hearing. But the artist knew, as we all did, that both to himself as interpreter and to the master he interpreted, our silence was a finer tribute than was all our noise. I think it is true that here, if ever, the full meaning of a great musical composition was grasped by a great number of people.

But just what was that meaning? What unaccustomed awareness was aroused in us who, learned and unlearned alike, stood mute with comprehension?

Pursued to its foundations, this is really a question of theory. It is one, therefore, which the musical theorists ought to be able to answer. But within the strict confines of musical theory the only answer I can find is essentially this: that the meaning of that music was neither more nor less than the meaning of structure, and that our exalted emotion was due to our having lived, for that brief moment, in a world of "pure" music, unrelated to and untainted by any of the ordinary realities of life.

9

This doctrine — whether out of diffidence in dealing with questions of aesthetics or out of a tacit respect for the long-established notion that music is the universal language — is implied rather than directly affirmed in the writings of most contemporary composers and critics. It is unequivocally stated, however, by no less a figure than Igor Stravinsky (in his *Chronicles of My Life*, 1936) who writes as follows:

I consider that music is, by its very nature, essentially powerless to *express* anything at all, whether a feeling, an attitude of mind, a psychological mood, a phenomenon of nature, etc. . . . *Expression* has never been an inherent property of music. That is by no means the purpose of its existence. . . . [Expression is] an aspect which, unconsciously or by force of habit, we have come to confuse with its essential being. . . . Music is given to us with the sole purpose of establishing an order in things, including, and particularly, the coördination between *man* and *time*. . . . Its indispensable requirement is construction. Construction once completed, this order has been attained, and there is nothing more to be said. (P. 83.)

Although it is difficult to reconcile this creed with the apparent purpose of many of Stravinsky's works, both earlier and later than this pronouncement, it seems to me to summarize, sufficiently for our purpose, the general concept of "pure" music. That he did not regard it as an over-statement is indicated in his description of the purpose of his *Symphonies of Wind Instruments*: "This music was not made to please nor to excite passions . . . It is an austere ceremony which revolves in brief litanies among the different families of homogeneous instruments."

These are the views of a composer. Samples of critical judgment in the same field may be noted from more recent works:

Leonard Meyer, in *Emotion and Meaning in Music* (Chicago, 1954), frankly recognizes not only the possibility but the fact of expressive communication. But his study — an admirably comprehensive exploration of the field of structure, especially in all its scientific aspects — goes little further into the wide field of extramusical expression than to affirm its existence.

Victor Zuckerkandl, on the other hand, in *The Sense of Music* (Princeton, 1959), not only explores as exclusively structural the tonal cohesions which we shall find capable of expressive intimation, but in the brief epilogue to his book speaks thus of the emotional communications we shall be concerned with:

And where, in all this, is there a place for *emotion*, which so many believe constitutes the very essence of music — so much so, in fact, that music is quite commonly referred to as the language of emotions?

There is just no place for emotion in the context of the essential question. Not because music can be divorced from emotion; it never can, there is no musical experience without emotion, that is to say, there is no way of grasping a musical context, the motion of tones, otherwise than by partaking in it, by inwardly moving with it — and such inward motion we experience as emotion. (P. 245.) *

But men look for meaning in anything they contemplate, and that meaning grows as the contemplated thing is found comparable with things like or unlike itself. The motion of music would be quite incomprehensible if it were not comparable to the already familiar motion of physical bodies. It is also comparable to the motion of our own bodies *under the stress of emotion* — so like it that, as we shall see, the musical portrayal of actual or even imagined bodily motion may be interpreted as a portrayal of the stress which generates that motion. To confine our contemplation of musical motion to the inner impulses of the musical body only is thus to put the imagination in jail.

But — although his ultimate conclusions are considerably different from ours — the expressive purpose of musical composition is also developed by an eminent contemporary composer from foundations precisely in accord with those which underlie the thesis of this book, as may be seen in the following quotations from Roger Sessions's *The Musical Experience* (Princeton, 1950):

"Since music is created by human beings, we must regard the sources, or raw materials, [rhythm and tone] first of all as human facts. For it is not rhythm and sound as such but their nature as human facts which concerns us." (P. 11.) Again, ". . . music is significant for us as human beings principally because it embodies movement of a specifically human type that goes to the roots of our being and takes shape in the inner gestures which embody our deepest and most intimate responses" (p. 19). And once more, ". . . what we may call the raw, formal materials of music are also the expressive elements, and these, again, have their basis

---

* Which is to say that although we "partake in" the emotion aroused by the musical substance as such (a participation we shall also explore), we must on no account recognize either the "motion of tones" (doubtless, Hanslick's *tönend bewegte Form*, which we shall also encounter) or those tonal stresses and cohesions which Zuckerkandl's book has minutely described as "the essential question," as in any way related to the emotions generated in us by non-musical experience. (His views are in some measure those of Heinrich Schenker.)

11

in certain of the most elementary, intimate, and vital experience through which we live as human beings" (p. 20).

What Mr. Sessions calls "inner gestures" are precisely the responses which we shall find elemental for expression. They will be rather minutely studied. But our preliminary investigations may now be resumed with a further examination of the experience communicated by our Bach concerto.

Indeed I am sure that the audience I have described, whose imaginations were unconfined, acclaimed a human as well as a purely musical interest in that concerto. (That they would hardly have interpreted the music in its pure aspect as revealing so obscure a fact as the coördination between man and time is beside the point.)That audience, moreover, was largely lacking in the knowledge and even in the experience of perfectly constructed musical form. If, then, the delight of pure music lies wholly in form, these humble listeners received much more than their due; for their formal learning was slight, but their pleasure was great. They behaved, at any rate, as if they had perceived expressive sense — meaning, that is, relative to the experiences and the emotions of life as they knew it — in the concerto. If, then, this meaning, as they perceived it, did not lie in the form or in the fact of pure tone relation indubitably exhibited in that concerto, whence did it come? Is there perhaps, not only in the finished fabric but in the elemental substance of music, some value which may be apprehended even by the unlearned but which is not, in the structural sense which musical theory intends, primarily a value of form?

This question offers a somewhat inexact but generally comprehensible statement of the problem we are to study — the problem of musical expression. And our orientation within the field of that problem may begin with a cursory examination of the elemental substance of music, to see how integral in that substance are the "impurities," as we may call them, that suggest other than purely musical contemplation to the listener.

The actual elements of music are tone and rhythm. Tone appears, in musical structures, in the guise either of melody or harmony (the latter being ordinarily reckoned as a third element of music); but in physical constitution these twain are one flesh. That flesh, as the physicist sees it, is a vibration in air — a vibration whose frequency and amplitude are measurable. No tone, however, that musicians use is physically "pure." All musical tone is a composite of fundamental and partial vibrations, of different frequencies and amplitudes. The ear, of course, does not recognize these attributes of tone in their physical aspect. It knows frequency as pitch, and amplitude as loudness. Moreover it ordinarily recognizes the mingling of a fundamental tone with its partials not as a complex but as a simple sensation-stimulus, and registers the sensation itself as one of tone *quality*. So interesting, however, is this fact of quality in tone that that term, as descriptive of the value of the sensation aroused, seems inadequate. Metaphorically, therefore, we call tone *quality* tone *color*; and so appropriate does this term seem that we are hardly aware that it is figurative — that a factually auditory sensation has somehow been transubstantiated into a visual.

Nor is color the only non-auditory impression to be aroused by the sensation of tone. With equal vividness, tones or harmonies appear to us as warm or sweet or hard or even fragrant. Visual, tactual, gustatory, and even olfactory imagery, that is, may be in some degree aroused by a stimulus reaching the mind through the ear alone.*

Since it is all but impossible to produce from any of our musical instruments a physically pure tone (i.e., one without overtones), no proponent of the theory of "pure" music demands that the musical fabric should be woven of such tone. And while such a theory may seem to ignore the quasi-synaesthetic interest of compound tone in principle, such tone, with its all but inevitable suggestion of more than tonal character, cannot be avoided in practice.† Thus it is evident that a reference to extramusical experience is in some measure not only perceptible in the formed substance of music but is demanded by its hearers.

Neither is tone the only musical element capable of arousing extramusical imagery. Rhythm, the other really elemental factor in musical structure, is far more suggestive. It is, indeed, by no means an element of music exclusively. It is fundamental for poetic and (in a more static guise) for graphic art as well, and is the abstract form in which motion is most clearly defined to consciousness. Factually, rhythm is exhibited as a pat-

---

* The intensity of these impressions is highly variable. Exceptional hearers report that they actually *see*, for example, the tone of the trumpet as red. The psychologist describes such a transfer as synaesthetic. This term is not strictly appropriate for the less vivid awareness we have described; but there is in any event an approach to that phenomenon.

† Stravinsky reproved Dr. Koussevitzky, after his first performance of the *Symphonies of Wind Instruments*, for having allowed or directed the musicians to play "expressively." Dr. Koussevitzky retorted that the expression he brought out was already in the notes. More than the one characteristic of tone we have so far noted was doubtless involved; but, whichever disputant was right, an intrinsic interest beyond that of pure structure seems indisputably present in music.

terned succession of points or moments of stress and non-stress. But the image which our minds immediately make out of such a succession is far more than an abstract pattern. Musical rhythm, particularly, is perceived as the very graph of motion — of a universally known, extramusical experience — and our actual awareness of rhythm, accordingly, is usually a considerably concrete presentation of motion imagery.

The rhythmic suggestiveness of music is probably greater than that of any other art — so great, indeed, that we all think of the substance of music as being in actual motion, and are surprised and not a little deflated when we realize that this substance, being incorporeal, cannot properly be said to move at all. The very insubstantiality of the musical substance, indeed, probably heightens greatly the interest of the motor suggestion, for it is not necessary that the motion depicted be that of some familiar moving body. The music of our concerto moved as does nothing in all the world outside music; yet we followed that motion as if it were the most convincing reality we had ever encountered, and much of our response to its appeal was a kind of spiritual enactment of the depicted motor fact.

Both tone and rhythm, then, considered merely as elements of musical structure, are intrinsically rich in extramusical suggestion. And if the hint of warmth or color conveyed by tone happens to complement the hint of motion conveyed by rhythm, so that the two suggestions, appearing simultaneously, seem to characterize a knowable fact of non-musical experience, then it is possible that an image of that experience will begin to emerge in consciousness as something portrayed, revealed, uttered, represented — in a word, as something *expressed* — through musical means. Other agencies, as well as amplifications of the suggestive value of tone and rhythm, will appear in the course of our study. But enough has been said to show the impossibility of constructing a theory of "pure" music without excising from the basic substances of musical structure many inherent qualities which are also evocative of extramusical interest.

I shall propose, in the sequel, a general theory of the process of musical expression. But I shall not defend that thesis effectively if I define vaguely the crucial word, expression. The quasi-synaesthetic suggestions just noted *are* suggestions evocative of feeling. But expression, in the proper sense of the word, is more than an awakening of feeling. It is the *intelligible* utterance, not merely of feeling but of thought; and to achieve expressiveness music must arouse both thought and feeling. It is true that a musical structure, viewed as purely as possible *as* structure, may awaken both.

14

But to maintain that purity of view, many intrinsic suggestions (such as those just noted) must be lopped of their feeling-foliage. And the thought and feeling generally implied in the word expression (and that with which this study is concerned) is that mingling of thought and feeling aroused by human, not by purely aesthetic experience.

I have insisted that there was conveyed by our Bach concerto a high awareness of human meaning. Without having set forth a theory of expression, I cannot demonstrate clearly my belief. Yet that same awareness was aroused, without the aid of any analytical demonstration whatever, in the audience that heard the concerto; and it may be of use to examine their awareness if only because it may yield a sharper understanding of the nature of that thought and feeling whose expression we are to study.

Our rapt attention during the performance was evidence that a process of thought was going on. The enthusiastic reception of the music was evidence, also, that feeling had been aroused. But it must be admitted that in neither of these facts is there any positive evidence that this feeling or this thought exceeded what may be called musical boundaries. For either those quasi-synaesthetic suggestions already discussed, or the more extensive implications still to be discussed, might have been so far submerged in immediate impressions of purely musical interest (and these were high) as to make the wider expressive import of the music negligible.

Neither can I remember any comments, after the performance, that indicated the nature or even the existence of extramusical perception. We agreed that the performance was marvelous; but that agreement did not comprise our whole impression. I should have protested, and I am sure that the audience would have protested with me, any interpretation of our experience that ignored or denied our perception of more than purely musical meaning in the concerto. I cannot, indeed, put that meaning into words. But that does not imply that there was no meaning. It implies only that I have no words whose meaning is commensurate with the idea conveyed by the music. I can, and I presently shall, indicate in words the general nature of the idea that we all, I am sure, found uttered there. But I shall not undertake even that verbal adventure until I have in some measure insured myself against bathos by showing how, in words as well as in music, meaning may sometimes be conveyed that is out of all proportion to the mere definitional sense of the vehicle that conveys the meaning.

No matter what the vehicle of expression, significant communications of idea are commonly achieved through the coherent presentation of

15

many contributory factual details. But in that culminant moment when we finally grasp the whole meaning, we cease to be concerned with the detail that has laid the foundation for our understanding. We see, in that moment, the "point" of the whole utterance. But that point, even when the medium of communication has been verbal, is an awareness no longer verbal. It is the perception of a full reality of experience — an awareness in which our every faculty of sensuous, intellectual, and emotional perception is indeed focussed to a point.

The only adequate verbal expression for such an awareness would be one single word; for the full perception of meaning often appears in the mind in an instant even shorter than the time it takes to utter a single syllable. Usually, of course, there is no such word. Sometimes, however, by careful preparation, a single word can be made amazingly to embrace and suggest the whole meaning of a highly involved experience. Othello, when at last Iago has insinuated into his mind the almost certain conviction of Desdemona's guilt, suddenly halts the outpouring of his rage and deepens our sense of his agony with the phrase, "The pity of it, Iago!" But this word, pity, as we ponder it, becomes big with meaning beyond definition. It sums up not only the whole hideous concatenation of event that led up to the moment of its utterance, but the intolerable pitifulness of the utterance itself, addressed to a mind incapable of pity. It has become feeling rather than knowledge — a pang of realization.

It was with such a pang as this that we grasped the sense of Bach's music. Its tones and rhythms had indeed set forth no facts to build up our sensitivity to that meaning. But there was reference to experience, nevertheless — to experience dimly understood and variously comprehended by every hearer; and no "purely" musical structure, seen without reference to that experience, could have assumed the dimensions of that pronouncement, gravid with meaning, which entered our minds with the stuff of that concerto. We were aware of a knowable reality — aware of it, not in words nor in images of tone nor in aesthetic sensibilities of structure and proportion, but in the very core and center of conviction where decision is made as to the truth or falsity of propositions that present themselves to the mind through experience. Somehow, this music spoke truth.

The truth of which this music spoke had already presented itself to us — originally, no doubt, through the senses, but ultimately in terms not of physical but of spiritual experience. I have no hesitation in asserting that the experience itself was one which we call by such names as faith and ecstasy. But whereas these words can but lamely suggest the spiritual condition derived from such experience, the music limned it with amazing vividness. These words, therefore, do not define the music. Rather, the music defined the words.

Music, then, is in its fullest function a definition of experience. So, indeed, is any other art. The range of any individual's immediate experience — his actual contact with the world — is so limited that if he were unable to communicate with his fellows, and to share in their discoveries, the range of his understanding would be pitifully limited. Art, therefore, communicates as well as defines experience. And music, to become a vehicle of communication, must operate in accord with other generally known and habitually utilized processes of thought. These musical processes — their basis and their functioning — are the chief object of our present inquiry.

But an art is also a craft of structure, addressed to sensibilities and perceptions capable of infinite refinement. That which satisfies these perceptions is ordinarily described as beautiful, and little favor will be accorded to that artistic effort which fails to conform to the prescription — whatever that may be — of beauty. Music, possessed of strong sensuous appeal, and capable of infinite variety in organization, is a strong contender for the favor of the lovers of beauty. But the achievement of beauty is difficult, and even if it demand no more than the attainments just mentioned, may well tax the skill of the artist — and for full realization the discrimination of the music lover — to its limit.

Yet, if music can attain to both beauty and expression it will appear as a more valuable offering than if it were possessed of either of these attributes alone. Both, in fact, are ordinarily demanded. But when both are present, the musical object becomes a much more difficult study, for the two values of beauty and expression, presented simultaneously, are hard to distinguish and to assay.

Our study, therefore, will begin with the problem of beauty as posed by the simultaneous offering of form and content. Next, the distinction between the two will be studied through observation of them in relation. Then, since form will have been seen to contribute significantly to expression, an attempt will be made to observe it in isolation. Content will be similarly studied for itself. And at last, against this clearer understanding of the essential components of the art-work, those factors of the musical

17

substance which are really elemental for expression will be identified and their functioning exhibited.

The preparation for this exhibit will seem over-long unless it is realized that our search is not merely for the fact of expression, which is apparent in much of the vast literature of music, but for the actual elements upon whose presence and whose normal functioning the fact of expression depends. These elements are of course present in that same musical substance which formal and structural analysis has long since dissected and described. They are not, however, visible in that analytical view, which has seemed to many — and particularly to the purists — to take account of all that actually exists in the musical substance. The discerning of the elements requires, therefore, a certain rectification of the conventional analytical focus; and for this a considerable preparation is needed.

The result of our inquiry will be a similar rectification of the current aesthetic view which is inclined to minimize the importance of musical expression or (as we have already seen) to deny its existence. This rectification, if our argument is sound, will be seen to follow, for the most part, as a natural conclusion drawn from the argument. One feature, however, will perhaps appear startling — the contention that music, which can at best but feebly represent things, is nevertheless like all the rest a representative art — the "object" represented being not the physical facts of experience which, to arouse emotional understanding, the other arts portray, but the emotions themselves which those facts arouse.

In any case, if music is really incapable of dealing intelligibly with the implications of vital experience, those who throughout its history have found it an expressive art have been deceived. Our discussion, then, is intended to enlarge the pleasure of the music lover by revealing an actual contact between music as a vehicle of communication and those regions of the mind where the meaning of experience is felt.

THE ELEMENTS

II

The Factors of Beauty

To those primitive satisfactions of physical appetite with which our evolution began, many new and more subtle delights have been added. As our experience grows, we become convinced that of all these the delight in beauty is the highest. Few, indeed, will readily confess insensibility to beauty. We even admit with a kind of shamefacedness any failure to respond to its appeal, as if our lapse were somehow a sin against the holy ghost. Yet, highly as we regard it, beauty remains a kind of mystery. We can neither define it as a positive attribute of an object nor describe clearly our reaction to an object we perceive as beautiful. Few, moreover, can profess complete responsiveness to every type of artistic appeal.

For there are many arts, and the response to any one of them requires an exceptional sensory endowment. It is either to the ear or to the eye that the highest artistic appeal is made; but the perceptive range of either of these organs is so wide that several distinct types of appeal, each forming a highly organized art, may be addressed to the mind through the single organ.

Yet all the arts, visual or auditory, have in common one ultimate purpose — the awakening of the sense of beauty. Diverse as they are in substance and subject matter, the awareness of beauty they arouse is itself almost undiversified; and we recognize this sense as an emotional experience of an altogether exceptional order. Our response to the thing of beauty, whatever may be its substance, is so instantaneous and our submission to its appeal is so complete that we seem not merely to know, but rather in our every sensibility to feel, its high significance. In comparison with this vivid awareness of both feeling and meaning, ordinary sensation or knowledge seems pale and glowless, and we are loth to admit that such precious moments are no more tangible than dreams.

We ponder, therefore, the delightful experience. But as we ponder it

21

the question, "What is beauty?" only becomes more perplexing. Instead of yielding an answer as compact and vivid as was our actual experience of beauty, the question becomes one of the most obscure and elusive of problems.

At first sight, however, this difficulty is not apparent. The source of our sense of beauty can hardly be other than the object — the work of art — whose contemplation creates that sense in us.* To study the substance, the structure, the finished surface of that work is thus naturally our first effort. We learn what we can of the artist's materials and his technique, hoping that the study of his constructive process will reveal the nature of his imaginative creation. If the beautiful thing we are studying is a piece of music, we may begin by analyzing the tones themselves and their physical composition. We shall account thus, in some degree, for their sensuous charm. Through detailed analyses of its melody and harmony and the other technically describable resources employed, we may account also for the coherence and the exquisite proportion of the whole created form.

But although we may seem thus to trace, even to its sub-conscious roots, each detail of the artist's *constructive* effort, his *creative* effort remains largely unexplained. For in the light of this structural and formal analysis merely, our response to the work is far less moving than was that vivid sense awakened by our original vision of the beautiful object. Beauty, it must then appear, is not wholly a fact of artistic substance, structure, and form.

Our response to this lesser value of form, however, like our fuller awareness of beauty itself, is emotion of an exceptional order. It is emotion aroused by a substance possessed of a high sensuous appeal; that substance is also so arranged as to offer the interest of an intricate and subtle pattern or form; and the sensuous values, by virtue of this organization, seem to be absorbed into the form itself and to heighten its interest. Such an object as this may readily command our whole attention, foreclosing our mind against any further critical effort.

If that effort be made, however — if we suspect that by attending to its form and substance alone we have failed to realize the beauty of an artwork to the full — then by comparing the pleasure of form with this fuller delight we may be able to discover in what respect the awareness of beauty is richer than the awareness of formal perfection.

* It is not contended, although it may here seem to be implied, that works of art are the only agents capable of awakening the sense of beauty.

The Factors of Beauty

Such a comparison will be more easily made if the art-work we are examining be a poem or a picture. For almost invariably our pleasure will then involve, in addition to the feeling evoked by perfected form, emotion of quite another order — emotion akin to that aroused in us by human as contrasted with artistic experience. The total area of our feeling is now far larger than that which was stimulated by the artistic substance as such. And if this awareness of human experience may properly be seen as fused with that of artistic form — which is itself a fusion of the awarenesses of substance and pattern — the principal components of the sense of beauty will seem to have been identified.

The objective of the artist — the would-be awakener of the sense of beauty — is thus to arouse two types of awareness: the one, *im*mediate — the direct response to the art-work as a fact of substance and form; the other, mediate — the indirect response to suggestions of experience not, in themselves, necessarily related to those offered by the form of the art-work as such. We may conveniently call these two values, respectively, form and expression, the word expression being understood in that sense of utterance or communication which we have already adopted. The word content is also acceptable as equivalent to expression.

The beautiful object, however, indisputably offers more to the mind than the mere additive sum of these two values. That excess, in any adequate definition of beauty, must be accounted for. No other factors than those of form and content seem identifiable. We must therefore attribute this excess of value to the fusion of the two. For at that moment when our contemplation of the art-work has brought full understanding — at that moment when we really experience the sense of beauty — we neither perceive form and expression as two separate entities nor desire to make any distinction between them. Our perception of each is blurred, but our awareness of their common significance is heightened.

The reader will have noted that our definition of content was based upon the examination of a hypothetical poem or picture — of a type of "representative" art whose reference to external, non-artistic experience was unmistakable. If the beauty of music (as we shall contend) is of the same order as that of the representative arts, it is evident that we must show some tangible relation, comparably intelligible as a reference to external experience, between the substance of music and that of the other arts. We have noted hints of such reference in the facts of tone quality and in the subtleties of musical rhythm. Even these (appearing, as they

23

do, in fusion) may arouse vague awareness of such non-musical "things" as love or death; the motion and the joy of the dance; the melancholy of grey twilight. But expressiveness comparable to that found in the representative arts is not offered by the musical substance as such. Is some medieval alchemy, some miracle of transubstantiation, to be invoked as the explanation of that fact of expressiveness without which music would have no history?

Our answer to that question will be found in the sequel. But there is another problem — a corollary to that of expression — which must arise if the value of expression in art is admitted. Reference to non-artistic experience is essential to expression. But, that reference being established, the question will follow, How significant is this experience, compared with other experiences, when both are seen as factors in the greater complexity of life? How far must an estimate of the value of a work of art depend upon the significance of the experience with which it deals? Has art, in the last analysis, a moral bearing?

That question likewise will be dealt with, in its musical aspect, in the sequel. Its import, however, which is not slight, may properly be indicated here. For while we are primarily concerned to identify the factors of beauty, we are also attempting to establish a basis of criticism, which is an estimate of value.

A distinction between good art and bad may of course be made on the basis of purely artistic accomplishment. The problems of artistic creation are so absorbing, and their solution so difficult, that the moral implications of the artists' work are often hidden, even from the artists themselves. Indeed, if to convey a moral lesson appears as the direct object of an artist's work, his endeavor will almost certainly prove a failure.* The artist's primary business is not to point a moral but to illuminate life. But if life, thus illuminated, appears as more than the mechanistic behavior of creatures somehow endowed with motility, irritability, and the power of reproduction, it cannot escape, when thought and imagination are added to those primitive endowments, a moral interpretation.†

* There are important exceptions. Milton's attempt to "justify the ways of God to man" is not an artistic failure.

† *The Kenyon Review*, in 1951, offered a symposium entitled "My Credo" which set forth the critical opinions on literary art of a number of eminent students. Among these was Douglas Bush of Harvard University. Toward his desire "for a fuller return to the broad and central road of criticism," he avowed his belief that "Unless literature is in its effect didactic . . . I do not know any sufficient reason for its ex-

The Factors of Beauty

If, then, the view of life and art as amoral be rejected as too facile, three objects will appear toward which a competent criticism of art must direct its attention — the essential content of the work (its subject); the treatment of that subject (its form); and finally the human significance of the whole (its ineluctably moral aspect). These implications in the problem of criticism are said to have been formulated by Goethe in the shape of three simple questions:

> What has the artist tried to do?
> How has he done it?
> Was it worth doing?

These questions offer an aesthetic rule-of-thumb which, since it comprises the three items of content, form, and human significance which we have discussed, may be taken as a fairly dependable statement of the essentials of criticism.

Their application to music, however, must present a difficulty. Until the content of music — its "subject," which in the other arts is normally an item or an aspect of non-aesthetic experience — becomes in some degree definable, we cannot answer the question, What has the artist tried to do? But until this first question is answered, the second cannot rationally be asked. Until you know *what* thing has been done, you cannot know *how* that thing has been done. And if you know neither what has been done nor how it has been done, it will be rash to decide whether it was worth doing.

The problem may of course be simplified by denying the relativity of art to non-artistic experience. If — as Stravinsky avers with regard to music, and as abstractionists often assert with regard to other arts — if art has nothing to do with the ordinary manifestations of life, then the answer to the question, What has the artist tried to do? will be, quite simply, To create a work of art. How he has done it will be determined by reference to accepted principles of art — principles formulated and understood by artists themselves. Similar criteria must determine the worth of the work. And the public, if it is to attain to true appreciation, must somehow be taught to abandon its inveterate expectation of finding in art a significant reference to life.*

istence, at least on the higher planes that we are here concerned with." Note the phrase, "in its effect."

* I hope it will be clear that I am here impugning not the work of the abstract artists, but the mistaken statements of their purposes, put forth by critics (and by

25

Patently, then, a valid criticism of music — and of the other arts — must depend in no small part on the just assessment of expressive significance in the art. If that significance is denied to music: if music is merely impressive, not expressive: if it has nothing to communicate as to the meaning of non-musical experience: then criticism can but precariously defend its claim to sisterhood with the other arts in their contribution to humanism. If, on the other hand, that power does exist, criticism can hardly be content with the general recognition (attested by the long historic association of music with humanism) of the expressive purport of music. It must demand a positive definition of expressive power.

Until the middle of the nineteenth century, no other evidence of a human meaning in music was demanded than its general recognition; but its existence was never denied. In 1854, however, Eduard Hanslick put forth his startling little book, *Vom Musikalisch-Schönen* (On the Beautiful in Music), which asserted that music was intrinsically incapable of expression, and that it was to be accepted and criticized solely as *tönend bewegte Form*. (The phrase is difficult to translate. "Form in tonal motion" is perhaps a fair suggestion of its meaning.) For the most part, the reaction was one of amazed incredulity. The book did serve, however, as a corrective of current, grossly exaggerated "interpretations" of music, and particularly of the inflated aesthetic doctrine put forth by the admirers of the "futurists." Hanslick's thesis was vastly solidified by Edmund Gurney in *The Power of Sound* (1880) — the most exhaustive treatise in the literature. Gurney's conclusions are essentially the same as Hanslick's; he finds no tangible feature of the musical substance which can account for expression; yet (in the present writer's view, inconsistently) he adduces endless examples of "good" music whose goodness is discernible, even by himself, only on the ground of the essentially humanistic exaltation they arouse.

The most intensive study of the question of musical expression in the earlier years of this century is doubtless Carroll C. Pratt's *The Meaning of Music* (1931). The foreword of that book announces the author's agreement with the views of Hanslick and Gurney; but the text itself often appears to contradict the foreword. Being a psychologist by profession, Professor Pratt looks to the laboratory for a corrective of unjust assumptions;

artists themselves) whose justifiable enthusiasm for their work distorts their critical judgment.

but even there he has found evidence of a positive nature in favor of expressive content in music. A brief quotation from a later article (in *The Journal of Psychology*, 1938, 5, pp. 149–156), entitled "Structural vs. Expressive Form in Music," will suffice to suggest his point of view:

> To say that music is the language of emotion does not mean that it *embodies* emotion. That is impossible. Emotions are bodily states, and bodily processes cannot be changed into sound. The *pattern* or form of bodily processes, however, can be duplicated in sound or in visual material. It is the similarity of pattern which leads us to the use of the same words for otherwise very different states. The composer who strives to give musical expression to his mood or emotion manages to discover and mould, presumably in most cases quite unconsciously, a tonal design which resembles very closely the internal pattern of his own affective state. *The music then sounds the way an emotion feels.* The character of such music is one aspect of its form, for some other form would give it a different character.
>
> This aspect of music, in order to distinguish it from purely structural analysis, might be called *expressive* form. . . . Not all musical expression is formal. But neither is all of it due to the emotions of the listener which are erroneously read into the music. . . . Studies have been made which show pretty conclusively that there is a definite nucleus of expression which is a property of the music itself. . . . It is the music which has these characteristics, not necessarily the listener.

Professor Pratt's proposition that there are two types of form, the structural and the expressive, is more than admission of the existence of musical expression. It is itself a theory of musical expression. In his brief article the theory of course remains undeveloped. It is thus perhaps unwise to comment critically on his proposal. But since we shall propose in the sequel another theory — one which will attempt to distinguish sharply the aesthetic value of form from that of expression — we can see only a dangerous confusion in his attempt to distinguish those values by assuming the existence of two opposed types of form, the structural and the expressive. One statement will serve to indicate the ground for our dissent. Professor Pratt contends that "the character of [expressive] music is one aspect of its form, for some other form would give it a different character." It is indubitable that changed form must entail changed character; but that does not prove that character is an aspect of form. For it may be argued with equal truth that "the form of expressive music is one aspect of its character, for another character would give it a different form."

We feel, accordingly, that every effort must be made to identify expressive values as distinct from values of form, and that terminology must be employed which, so far as is possible in this difficult distinction, is free from ambiguity. The following chapter will reveal something of the difficulty involved, which appears even when the medium of expression is verbal, not musical.

❧ *III* ❧

Form and Content in Relation

W E H A V E seen that our awareness of beauty appears to be compounded of two lesser perceptions — those of form and content. Analysis reveals no other factors in the beautiful object; yet the sum of these two, valued purely in their analytical aspect, is less than the whole value apprehended in the thing of beauty. We must assume, accordingly, that the sense of beauty is somehow awakened by the fusion of these two contributory factors in the one comprehensive awareness. To examine the fact of fusion itself will thus be our first task.

Before that fact can be profitably studied, however, the things fused must be as clearly identified as possible. With music, such identification is exceptionally difficult. The fact of form appears to be clear, but the fact of content is extremely obscure. In poetry, on the other hand, the two components are more clearly differentiable. Poetic form is a tangible aesthetic value; poetic content, residing partly in the definitional meanings of words, is to that extent unmistakable. That the two, in fusion, may awaken the sense of beauty can hardly be denied. We shall therefore take for illustration and study of the fact of fusion a single stanza from a little song of Tennyson's, so familiar that its earlier portions will not need to be recalled by quotation:

> Ah, sad and strange as in dark summer dawns
> The earliest pipe of half-awaken'd birds
> To dying ears, when unto dying eyes
> The casement slowly grows a glimmering square;
> So sad, so strange, the days that are no more.

The general form is to be seen in the five-lined stanza with its iambic meter and its lack of rhyme — a pattern of structure which might have been used for the expression of many other types of idea, and which may

29

thus be set down as a purely artistic fact. Yet this very absence of all poetic device is of a certain expressive value, since it does not force upon us any extraneous consciousness of poetic design in the midst of our contemplation of the idea.

The content or idea — similarly in general outline — is difficult to reduce to its bare essentials as idea; but for the sake of our experiment we may attempt to state it as a comparison of the bitterness of our fading memory of former days with the bitterness of a dying man's fading vision of the living world.

But in the poem itself, neither form nor idea is the lifeless object our words have suggested. There is here the vivid image of a scene of death and a high imaginative suggestion of its meaning as a human experience. And this is accomplished by subtle management of the details of both idea and form — by the selection of particularly significant features of the scene for the suggestion, and by skillful arrangements of syntax and verbal sound for the utterance, of the poetic idea.

Unless we pause to consider it, we shall hardly realize the artist's skill in choosing his images. There is here no horrid catalogue of the apparatus of death. Dim light; silence; the awakening, without, of life that is all indifferent to the dwindling of life within — these "things" alone are offered for our contemplation. They are small indeed in magnitude in proportion to the vision evoked; but they are compelling because each image contributes to the awakening of a strong instinct of mystery, sympathy, or fear, and because no irrelevant encumbrance of merely poetic ornament or detail is allowed to impede that awakening.

Thus far we have considered idea rather than form, although we cannot deny that the careful selection of the images — and, as we shall soon observe, their placement — is itself a fact of form.

Our feeling, as we read, is however by no means wholly stimulated by these objective images. Values of verbal sound and of rhetorical arrangement add incalculably to our awareness of meaning in them. But as we observe this minuter detail we shall begin to be uncertain whether we are dealing with values of form or values of content.

Taking the sound-values first, observe the careful distribution, and in the three middle lines the suppression, of the sibilants: eleven sharp s-sounds only, in the fifty-two syllables of thirty-nine words. Seven of these sibilants occur in the first and last lines, where the emotional tide is less high and where the alliterative emphasis they offer gives a certain formal interest to these words of lower emotional altitude. The other four are more definitely expressive in their palpable intensification of the strange hush of that last earthly moment that confronts us. The *s* in *earliest*, appearing in the swifter motion of this anapaestic foot, and in immediate relation to the singular shortness of the long *i* in *pipe*, makes these words almost onomatopoeic. The next line has no sibilant whatever, so that the three in the following line (*the casement slowly grows a glimmering square*), grouped with the darkest vowels, serve to keep the heaviness of these vowels from becoming overweighted. (*Window*, instead of *casement*, would have overloaded the line intolerably.)

Nasals and dentals are similarly distributed for the enrichment of the sound; the vowels grow broader and deeper as the curve of the long sentence droops; and the rhythmically redundant syllable in *glimmering*, after the two darkest vowels, causes the long-delayed cadence to "tremble away into silence" with the fading of the vision itself. Such handling of verbal tone as this is an art of sound, almost as much as music itself. Its heightening of the verbal sense is indescribable.

But again, these sound-values are only details in a larger design — the curve of the syntax. The pattern of the sentence, not merely as pattern but as a correlative of the sense conveyed, is extraordinarily suggestive. There is first given (in the words *Ah, sad and strange*) a hint of somber circumstance of whose nature we are as yet unaware.* In the next words (*as in dark summer dawns*, etc.) the scene is slowly unveiled; but only after this gradual illumination of the background we are allowed to glimpse (in the words, *to dying ears*) the central figure in the scene of death. The prominence now given to that figure is heightened both by repetition of the word *dying*, and by the reiteration of the long i-sound (now become characteristic, almost as if it were a musical leading-motive) in the following word, *eyes*. And now, from this the highest altitude of the curve of

---

* The word *strange*, indeed, has a value not perceptible except in relation to the preceding stanza:

> Fresh as the first beam glittering on a sail
> That brings our friends up from the underworld,
> Sad as the last which reddens over one
> That sinks with all we love below the verge;
> So sad, so fresh, the days that are no more.

In the last line, *sad* and *fresh* appear in the opposite order to that in which they were first mentioned. This inversion is no accident, for *sad*, by beginning the stanza we are studying, gains a cumulative intensity, and *strange* now stands in sharp antithesis to *fresh*. The five thickening consonants in *strange*, surrounding the one long vowel, also give that word an extraordinary foreboding force.

thought, there is completed a striking inversion (begun with the repetition of *dying*) of the careful crescendo of suspense with which the climax was approached. The rest of the long sentence — in form and sound a musical *diminuendo* — leads at last into the very core of that somber feeling which, with the word *strange*, first aroused our interest and our dread.

There is here, indubitably, form — both in sound and thought. So intimately do the values of sound coincide with the values of sense that at first sight it seems impossible to distinguish them positively as of the one order or the other. Also, it is only with their coincidence that the full sense of beauty is brought home to us. We are almost ready to say that in this verse form and expression are not merely coincidental but are identical.

Indeed, the notion is widely held that in any true work of art form and content are identical. The abstractionists in contemporary poetry and painting seem to adopt it, and even with reference to classic painting the idea was stoutly maintained by such writers as Clive Bell and Roger Fry.* It appeals especially to musicians. The absence — indeed, the impossibility — of any reference, in the substance of great instrumental compositions, to facts or conditions of human experience, as well as the high absorption of the hearer in the tonal substance itself, gives the notion a peculiar plausibility.†

But a moment's consideration will show that this proposition — the statement that form and expression are identical — is a verbal absurdity. The word form means shape and organization. Expression means utterance. To say, then, that form and expression are identical is to say that these words are synonyms — that "form" means "utterance," and "expression" means "shape." No advantage — unless a certain delight in the miraculous — can accrue from such reasoning.

* Bell tried valiantly to establish a distinction between "formal form" and significant form," but appears, at last, to have abandoned it. This distinction seems to the writer as untenable as Professor Pratt's differentiation between structural and expressive form — essentially on the same grounds.

† Walter Pater's idea (set forth in *The School of Giorgione*) that all the arts strive to attain to the condition of music because in it the values of form and content *are more completely blended* than elsewhere, has been gratefully quoted — and at the same time misinterpreted as an assertion of actual identity — by many writers on music. For that assertion, plausibly stated, will seem to imply a certain superiority of music over all the other arts in the matter of spirituality. This superiority being acknowledged, a similar elevation must follow of the musician over other artists.

But it is quite possible that the musician's self-exaltation is really the ground upon which the notion of the superiority of his art is based. Closed circles of devotees are often composed of circular reasoners. But the viciousness of a circle is not lessened by the fact that its arc is so wide as to appear a straight line.

Form and Content in Relation

To say that form and expression cannot be identical is not, however, to say that they are immediately distinguishable. These two values, most subtly blended, are evident in our illustrative stanza. If music is actually an expressive art, they must be present in music also. They will there be even more difficult to distinguish. Yet any final clarity in criticism must depend upon such distinction. Thus it will be useful to examine our stanza further, in the hope of finding there a dependable understanding of their relation. For it is probable that the principle underlying the relation we may find there will hold in the case of music also.

We have in the stanza a mixture of form and expression or idea. To take away one component from a mixture of two is ordinarily to leave the other. If then we can destroy the form of our stanza without destroying its idea, a comparison of the transformed stanza with the original should give a more exact measure of the dimension and the importance of the factor of form. This may be done — approximately but by no means precisely — by turning the language of the verse into the following prose form:

Like the days that are no more, to dying ears the half-awaken'd birds' earliest pipe in dark summer dawns is strange and sad while slowly the casement grows a glimmering square to dying eyes.

What is lost? Impressiveness of sound, vividness of imagery, and with them every vestige of the sense of beauty. The idea itself has also shrunk into insignificance. Words that in the poem bulged with meaning have dwindled to their barest conversational sense. Yet the factual substance of the idea — at least in so far as that idea inheres in the definitional sense of words — is retained; for the purport is the same, and only inessential words have been omitted or altered. If so much or so little can be conveyed by different arrangements of the same words, it is evident that not only aesthetic interest but also a great wealth of meaning must itself either reside in or depend upon form.

This is not, however, an immaterial alternative. For to say that the idea of this stanza — or rather, that portion of the idea which was destroyed in our experiment — *resides in* the form is to say that form and idea are not only indistinguishable but are in a very real sense identical. On the other hand, to say that idea *depends upon* form is to pose a very different problem. For to the extent to which this dependence can be established, the distinction between form and idea will itself be established.

The stanza, incontestibly, was beautiful by virtue of the presence within

33

it of form and meaning. Incontestibly also, by destroying the form of the stanza we destroyed much meaning resident in the stanza. But does it necessarily follow that the meaning we destroyed *resided in* the form we destroyed?

The poetic form disappears in the prose version. But a considerable fraction of the original meaning still remains — that part which resided in the words taken merely as definitional symbols, and also a portion of that which was conveyed by intelligible syntax. This remainder of bare definitional and syntactical meaning did not, accordingly, reside in the poetic form. The meaning we destroyed must therefore have been a poetic increment of meaning — a bulging of verbal sense (and of poetic imagery) somehow attributable to poetic form. But did this increment reside in, and thus become an integral part of, the poetic form? Did form and idea become identical?

Although the proposition of identity, thus presented, may appear more plausible, it is as absurd as ever. For there is no essential difference between a poetic increment of meaning and the original definitional sense of a word thus augmented. Both are primarily definitional in character. The word *strange*, for example, in its poetic position, cannot be (as it often is in conversation) equivalent merely to "odd." It strikes a definite note of foreboding, of dread, of the imminence of catastrophe. But this is still an increment of *meaning* — an increment indubitably *effected* by form, but inconceivable without the primary symbolism resident in the word. The alliterative sibilants in *sad* and *strange* contribute pointedly to this heightened sense. The alliteration between *dark* and *dawns*, in the same line, seems far less significant. Yet both, considered purely as facts of form, are of equal value. Their difference, then, is a fact of borrowed meaning, not a fact of form. Thus there is no evidence in our stanza that meaning — understood as a reference to external experience — resides in form, or is conceivable as identical with form. It is equally evident, however, that the artistic substance through which meaning is conveyed must have form; and to discover that form which is most appropriate to the meaning to be conveyed is a major artistic problem.

This appropriateness — patently achieved in our stanza — is thus a blending of the values of form and meaning. In that blending, the margins of form and the margins of meaning overlap. To the apprehending mind, the two values thus appear in a fusion so complete that awareness of the two as individual entities is obscured and sublimated in the higher awareness of beauty. But the two are still entities, incapable of transubstantiation. And if music has meaning, as we shall contend, a just critical estimate of musical value must rest upon a discrimination, as clear as possible, of these two entities within the musical substance.

The analogy just suggested will doubtless seem strained to the breaking-point. No such precise symbolism may be predicated of music as the (supposed) one-to-one relation of the verbal symbol with the thing symbolized.* But — as our stanza has amply shown — the actual communication offered by words when they are used in their highest evocative sense is vastly more comprehensive than can be accounted for by one-to-one symbolization. And the meaning of music, as we glimpsed it in our Bach concerto and as we shall see more clearly when the process of musical expression has been explored, is chiefly to be found within this area of intuitive perception. It will be found, however, to be based upon the actual representation — as vivid as the symbolism of words — of our normal feeling response to "things." And while our awareness of "things" will prove to be largely intuited from the music rather than directly perceived in it, the final communication will be indubitably rooted in that extramusical experience whose meaning it is every man's constant effort to interpret.

The value of our stanza, criticized in the light of the three simple questions quoted above, is considerable. Not only was the thing to be done well done. The whole effort was worth while because it illuminated an experience generally stamped as significant. But the manner of its doing naturally took most of our critical attention, for a clumsy or deficient technique would have reduced the effort to insignificance. The form of the stanza is admirable. Yet that form was not created for its own sake. Its details were chosen and applied to the larger creative purpose, not because they were clever, nor because the sound-sequences and the syntactical curve were artistic objectives in themselves, but because these things were suited, as no others among the thousand devices at the command of the poet were suited, to the expression of this idea and no other.

In itself, however, technical manipulation, whether of words or tones

* The Wagnerian leading-motive, by more or less legitimately pre-establishing such a relation, does approximate to an almost verbal definiteness of reference. But it does this — and can do it — only through an artificial (but not unnatural) association with words or with verbal concepts. The whole art of song — the most ancient species of music — has borrowed thus from verbal imagery. It fails, also, when that borrowing has been misconceived. But that failure could not be discovered if there were no intrinsic musical meaning to compare with the verbal.

or colors, is a difficult and absorbing task — so difficult that it often demands the artist's whole store of energy for its mastery. Even when the objective of expression is itself of little moment, imposing surfaces may be contrived for its utterance, and through such a display of skill the apparent worth of the structure may be inflated far beyond the value which a sober judgment will set upon it. Compare, in this light, the stanza we have been studying with the following, from Swinburne's "The Mill Garden":

> Stately stand the sunflowers, glowing down the garden side,
> Ranged in royal rank arow along the warm grey wall,
> Whence their deep disks burn at rich midnoon afire with pride,
> Even as though their beams indeed were sunbeams, and the tall
> Sceptral stems bore stars whose reign endures, not flowers that fall.
> Lowlier laughs and basks the kindlier flower of homelier fame,
> Held by love the sweeter that it blooms in Shakespeare's name,
> Fragrant yet as though his hand had touched and made it thrill,
> Like the whole world's heart, with warm new life and
>   gladdening flame.
> Fair befall the fair green close that lies below the mill!

Superabundant alliteration, strained figurative imagery and all the mechanics of poetic artistry are manifest — too manifest. We need not weary ourselves with examination of this verse. Swinburne, to paraphrase a saying of Goldsmith's, has made his Sweet Williams talk like orchids.

This chapter should have established as essential to the awareness of beauty the fact of fusion in our perception of the two principal components of that awareness — the form of the utterance and the meaning (illuminated by that form) of the experience involved. The sense of beauty, then, appears as a heightened comprehension of experience — a pang of realization, striking, not merely in the region stimulated by the art-work as a phenomenon of color, sound, or whatever, nor merely in that region where experience is cognized, but also, and predominantly, where the meaning of experience is felt.

That music can awaken this sense is abundantly testified by its history. Few ears are so dull that they cannot distinguish a dirge from a dance; and the history of music is a record of progressively finer distinctions. Not *whether* music can achieve expression, but *how* it achieves it, is our problem. For if the components of the sense of beauty in music are essentially the same as those which we have found in our stanza — if form, in great

art, does not exist in and for itself but for the illumination of experience —
then an examination of both form and content as they appear in the musical art-work may lead to the discovery of those factors of the musical
substance which are really elemental for expression.

Our next chapter, accordingly, will examine the fact of musical form
and the implications resident and discernible in it.

❦ *IV* ❦

Form in Isolation

THE foregoing will have revealed something of the interdependence of form and meaning in awakening the sense of beauty. A single unit of poetic structure (a word) may possess the value either of form or of meaning; and that unit appears in a considerably different guise accordingly as it is observed in the one aspect or the other. But when these values are fused — when such an art-work as our illustrative stanza is viewed in its normal perspective — not only that unit but the whole art-work itself possesses a higher interest than when either its formal or its expressive aspect is considered alone. Fusion of this sort thus credibly appears as an important source of that value commonly called beauty.

It should be noted that we made no attempt to establish the relative weight or volume of either form or meaning in the stanza. Indeed the two values are so different that no common scale can be devised upon which to measure the strength of their appeal. Thus a precise definition of beauty — a term which is nevertheless a coin in every man's cash-box of verbal symbols for experience — has never been acceptably formulated. Yet the two words, form and meaning — our names for the two principal contributors to the fact of beauty — do evoke two distinct mental images. They symbolize two distinct entities, whose distinction fusion cannot obliterate. (The two words, as we have seen, refuse to become synonyms.)

To study each of these fused components of the art-work in isolation — so far as they can be isolated — would thus appear to be a profitable effort. But we must recognize that this proposal is figurative. "Form," as a symbol for the product of organization, seems a factual term. "Meaning" is also, if more doubtfully, acceptable as factual. But the fusion we so glibly imagined is not effected in a similarly factual crucible. It is effected in the mind; and the "things" — form and meaning — suggested by these names are

38

not the external facts which we momentarily supposed those terms to symbolize. They are our mental images of these things; and their fusion is the fusion not of these things but of their images.

Moreover, none of these images, however sharp and factual, is merely the image of the thing contemplated. That image is formed in *my* mind, and in the general perspective of *my* interest; and the scale upon which it is measured is the scale of its value *for me*. My scale of values is provided by that store of experience which I have accumulated through contact with other objects comparable with this immediate one. My awareness of that object — my "idea" of it — will vary with the competency and the sharpness of my attention to the detail of the object, and with the depth of that contribution drawn from my store of experience. Thus — however precarious the adventure to the eye of the philosopher — it appears possible to define an idea as at once *a mental image and a valuation of experience.**

The image may be vivid or faint (for example, an imminent physical danger, or an imagined portent); it may be concrete or abstract (the joyous reunion with a friend, or the end of the cold war); it may be persistent (an obsession) or evanescent (a fleeting awareness of color or odor); but an idea not rooted in an image of experience will be far to seek. The valuation of that image will ordinarily arouse a far larger volume of mental excitement than does the image itself, viewed merely as image. The value may, of course, be so slight that the image itself is at once dismissed. But even this insignificance is assessed (sometimes mistakenly) in the light of the self's constant care for its own well-being; that same self-interest will be interjected (perhaps quite unconsciously) into the more complex valua-

* The scientist of course forms his image with the utmost care for the rejection of his personal valuation of it. He tests it in his laboratory by methods scrupulously designed for this elimination, seeking, through his own effort and through his borrowing from the experience of his colleagues, to form a factual valuation of a factual image. In the light of his method his conclusions appear — and in their application outside the laboratory often prove — to be incontrovertible.

Yet the "thing" upon which he experimented had to be prepared before it could be examined in the laboratory. So prepared (e.g., by killing a living thing, and so altering its aspect as a living thing), that thing was thus inevitably shaped for interpretation according to the pre-established laboratory method in whose light it was examined. His conclusions, therefore, were to some extent pre-established by the method pursued in reaching them. The scientist will say that his conclusions are not his, but those of Science. Yet he does not wholly evade the personal equation, for his conclusions are also his, the Scientist's. And a good deal of experiment, in the field of musical psychology particularly, seems amply to justify Alfred North Whitehead's comment that, after all, "experiment is only a method of cooking the facts."

tions of weightier images; and in consequence the valuation-factor of idea will prove to be, in variable and incalculable degree, emotional.

Thus our effort to isolate and assess the component of form in the artwork is by no means simple. For the *fact* of form (its image), apparently definable as a composite of structural details, is not the *reality* of form as our mind, out of its store of experience, values it. That reality is not only *perceived* as a coherent structural composite and judged for the nicety with which its parts (whose sensuous substance may here be of high import) are adjusted to each other; it is *felt*; and that feeling is an integral factor in our whole awareness of form.

In that idea of form which we are now trying to isolate, the image of experience will be that of the artistic substance and its organization. The valuation of that image — vastly more complex — will be an assessment of the cohesions which bind together the units of the form and of the forces which bring about cohesion; of the resultant fact of design and its import as design; and of the artistic substance itself as adaptable to design and contributory to its fuller import. We noted, even in the substance of music (perhaps the purest of all artistic substances), the presence of certain "impurities" which awoke inevitable association with non-musical experience. Such extraneous suggestion (doubtless also intrinsic in other artistic materials and procedures) will be, as far as possible, ignored.*

To facilitate our study of form and content in relation, we took as our object a poetic "thing." We must now examine a more difficult object: a musical "thing" — or rather, *the* musical thing in general, seen in its structural aspect. Seen as a whole, this object may be viewed as static — that is, as a fact of pure design. But our image will be more accordant with the whole purpose of its organization if we view it, with Hanslick, as a *tönend bewegte Form.*

To any competent image of musical form, many minute details must contribute. The enumeration of these — often, in themselves, obvious musical facts — will be tedious and repellent. But they need to be recalled in order that our image of form, whether in its dynamic or its static aspect,

---

* Purity in abstract design appears to be sought (but hardly attained) through similar exclusion. I was once conducted through the work-rooms of an art school by an instructor who showed, among other problems posed for the students, several background-rectangles of neutral grey upon which were superimposed smaller squares of white. Each white square was poised, more or less precariously, on one of its corners. The problem was to assess the degree of tension aroused in the observer by each of the squares. I feel sure that the instructor was a little disturbed when I suggested that the real source of the tension was our awareness of gravitation.

may be as clear as possible. For the valuation of that image — the emergent idea of form — will depend largely on the accuracy of our observation of these details.

The original sense-experience out of which the concept of musical form is built up is the sensation of tone. Tones have three principal characteristics — pitch, timbre, and intensity. Each of these qualities contributes significantly to the musical form whose image we are trying to construct; but to the "black-and-white" outline of form, pitch and intensity are the chief contributors.

Pitch-judgment, in musical practice, is a discrimination of considerable nicety. Through the exercise of this judgment choice has been made of the tones most contributory to melodic interest and harmonic compatibility. The orderly succession of tones, thus selected, is of course our scale. Its history is far too long and intricate for attempted summary here. Our present scale — established, like our language, by many varied practical selections — contains no interval smaller than the half-step. In its "tempered" form it consists exclusively of multiples of that interval. The half-step seems to be the smallest interval which can be accurately discriminated by the general ear. It is not found in the primitive, usually pentatonic, scales, and seems to have become rather slowly appreciable by the generality of listeners during recorded musical history. Even in the twentieth century, little effort has been made to extend the general discrimination to the quarter-tone, but the newer harmonic vocabulary will perhaps come to include this interval as a regular rather than an exceptional feature. Out of these scale-tones all our musical form-patterns are built up.

Since the tones forming a pattern must appear in succession, discriminations of time as well as of pitch must enter into the image of musical form. The principal time-factor in musical patterns — obviously not "purely" musical — is rhythm. This is perceived as a symmetrical succession (possibly spatial as well as temporal) of instants or points of alternate stress and non-stress. A rhythmic image may be aroused, without other suggestion of stress, merely through the recurrence of similar or striking features of a pattern at the appropriate moment of time (as in music or poetry), or at the appropriate point in space (as in painting or architecture); but in music, rhythm is mostly made manifest through the third of the important characteristics of tone mentioned above — that of intensity.

The "black-and-white" image of musical pattern may be fully suggested by the values of pitch and rhythm. The value of timbre is thus largely incidental (rather than fundamental) to design, but — like the manifold variety of a well-modulated speaking voice — it illuminates the syntax and enriches the rhetorical contrasts of the texture. It blends so appropriately with the factors of pitch and rhythm as to be, in any sensitive performance, all but indistinguishable from them. Indeed, in some of the music of Debussy, and more notably in that of Anton von Webern, timbre seems to attain the status of an actual element of design. Pitch and rhythm, however, chiefly provide the bony structure of musical organizations.

Pitch — or, more accurately, tone of acceptably identifiable pitch — is obviously the one "physical" component of the musical substance. We have seen that our scale is the series of tones, arranged in the order of their pitch, which have been found acceptable for the organizing of musical patterns. But the scale is more than a mere pitch-succession. It is itself a tonal organization, having — palpably to the general ear — a beginning-tone and a notably similar ending-tone an octave distant from it.*

This beginning- and ending-tone is an object of high import. For it perceptibly governs the whole series as a tonic or key-note, possessing a central gravitational attraction for all the notes of the series. Earlier musical systems (such as the Gregorian Modes) exhibited tonal gravitation otherwise centered, less patent, and less powerful; our own system has shown an extraordinary widening of the tonal orbits; but all musical cohesion seems to rest, in one degree or another, on the presence — at any given moment, but for no prescribable time thereafter — of a central gravitational tone. Our study will for some time be confined to that music in which tonality (this gravitational force) is unmistakable.†

---

* The "identity" of two tones an octave apart is easily *described* in terms of their vibration-ratios. Other intervals are similarly measurable. But neither the identity of octaves nor the consonance or dissonance of other intervals is *explained* by these mathematical facts. Consonance and dissonance, for the ear, are simple sensation-values.

This fact appears too elementary for discussion — until new schemes of organization are proposed which would abandon the distinction between consonance and dissonance as too elementary for tolerance — e.g., the general theorem of atonality. That theorem no longer holds. And its rejection probably rests on the fact that tones possessed their present vibration-ratios long before there were human ears to hear them; those ears evolved in that tonal environment and were physically adjusted to it; and the organization of our scale reflects that adjustment. (The reader will see in Chapter XI that this comment does not imply a theoretical rejection of "modern" music.)

† The gravitational tendencies of the notes of our scale are indicated in the names given them in classical theory: (1) Tonic; (2) Super-tonic; (3) Mediant; (4) Sub-dominant; (5) Dominant; (6) Sub-mediant; (7) Leading-tone. The Leading-tone "leads toward" the Tonic. The Dominant's function is felt when that tone is the

Form in Isolation

Out of this primary gravitational "pull" grows another functional relation, chiefly observable in melody, between the notes of the scale. In melodic progressions, the notes of the tonic chord (as C–E–G in the key of C) appear as "rest-tones," while all the others, chromatic or diatonic, are felt as "active," having a tendency to move to the nearest rest-tone. This tendency will appear highly significant when we come to examine the expressive functions of musical tones; but it is also important for "pure" structure.

The hearer ordinarily finds the outline of musical form in the melodic line, or in some similar thread of continuity into which he compacts the sense of the thicker harmonic substance. Far more of that pattern than he realizes, however, is shaped for him by harmony. This resource, unknown to the ancients, was developed — very slowly at first — within historic time. It has proved to be the most significant of all the forces contributing to design. It gives a third dimension to the otherwise two-dimensional substance of melody; it yields endless subtleties of color and inflection, and makes possible those contrasts of mass and weight without which such a formal structure as the symphony would be unthinkable.

The sensory awareness upon which harmonic perception builds is that of concord and discord — values patently akin to those of rest and activity in melodic tones. Harmony incalculably subtilizes and enriches these values, since rest-tones may be harmonized by discord and active tones by concord. The propulsive force of concord is slight, even when conjoined with active melodic tones; but rhythmic propulsion is not necessarily impeded by concord. Since there are but two purely concordant harmonies (the major and minor triads), discord (which may exhibit endless degrees of harshness) is almost incessant, yielding an impression of activity illimitably varied. "Form in tonal motion" may thus become a high reality.

Still another enlivening factor — rhythm — permeates the whole tonal substance. Rhythm, however, is not only a vitalizer. Its pattern, freely alterable, is clearly "visible" as a contribution to design, even when design is viewed in its static aspect. But its kinetic energy, applied to the

foundation of that harmony (e.g., G–B–D in the key of C) which most strongly indicates the centrality of the Tonic. "Sub-dominant," however, does not mean "the note under the Dominant." It is *another* Dominant, a 5th *under* the Tonic, as the (upper) Dominant is a 5th *above* it. The two Mediants (midway-tones), in this light, become quite rational. The intervening "chromatic" notes are modifications (colorings) of the diatonic notes. Thus F♯ is a species of F, and in musical meaning quite different from G♭, its "enharmonic." The proper "spelling" of music is almost as essential to clear sense as is the same convention for language.

resources of activity in melody or harmony, may yield a pattern whose dynamic interest is in the last degree compelling. It is evident that the composer, commanding all the resources just described, has ample material for the creation of an infinite variety of structural patterns.

A successful pattern — in music as truly as in dress — is certain to be imitated. A widely imitated pattern thus becomes a convention, joyfully adopted by the uninventive. The many forms of music described in the books on music appreciation are such patterns. Their over-all design and its contributory details, studied minutely and set forth in the language of musical Emily Posts, become the rules which guide the imitators. Form, in this guise, becomes the problem and the product of manufacture. To the mind schooled in the convention, this product, skillfully made, is hard to distinguish from the artist's creation; for even the created thing had originally to be made by hand, and by that same skill which the artist has taught to the manufacturer.

The difference is indeed beyond description. It cannot be found either in the large outlines of conventional form-patterns such as sonata, rondo, passacaglia, or fugue, nor even in the observance, in those patterns, of the classic aesthetic principle of unity in variety. It lies, somehow, in the adjustment of the basic units of musical structure to the attainment of that final coherence and lucidity which appears in the ordering of all convincing thought. Yet description of those units and their more elementary organization may be attempted.

The smallest unit of musical structure is the motive. This is a group of two or more notes, usually observed as a fact of melodic succession, although a striking harmony or a distinctive rhythmic antic may be its most characteristic feature.* Successions, either of the same motive repeated or of contrasted motives, make up larger form-units called phrases; phrases similarly expand into clauses and clauses into sentences and periods (paragraphs) — the whole continuity thus resembling closely the general pattern of linguistic discourse, with perceptible punctuations called cadences (half, partial, deceptive, or full). While our apparently intuitive expectation of rhythmic symmetry is often literally met, unrelieved symmetry

* The following will serve as examples: of melodic motive, the four descending notes beginning the main theme of Beethoven's piano sonata, Op. 10, No. 3; of rhythmic motive, the three-note figure that opens Mozart's symphony in G minor (No. 40); of harmonic motive, that strange equivalent (in sound but not in meaning) of the minor triad, "spelled" C–D♯–G, which, with its unexpected resolution, serves as a kind of "Fate-motive" in Wagner's *Ring of the Nibelungs*.

becomes a fault (resembling the tedium of scansional reading in verse) which is often avoided by ingeniously adding to or subtracting from the expected sum of $(2 + 2) + (2 + 2)$ measures which makes up the "normal" period.*

While this rhythmic regularity is ordinarily found in the musical substructure — in what may be called the rhythmic piers upon which the formal design rests — the superstructure may exhibit endless variety. Musical textures are seldom woven so simply as to present, against the warp of even or symmetrical measure-groups, a single strand merely of woof in the shape of motive sequence or melody. The harmonic substance of music is of several strands (voices); it may be figurated (made into individual patterns closely resembling motives); and it may include completely formed melody, either subordinate in interest to the main thought or co-ordinate with it. Larger divisions may likewise exhibit similarity or contrast of pattern, cohesion being achieved by emphasis on already familar features, often combined in new ways. Repetition, with contrast of key or more extensive development of thematic material, serves the purpose of recall or of summation. Sound musical discourse, indeed, whether in one conventional form-pattern or another, will be found to fulfill Aristotle's formula — elaborated by long-winded analysts for two thousand years, but still comprising the essence of rhetorical common sense — that a discourse should have a beginning, a middle, and an end. For this is indeed the pattern of clear and convincing thought, in whatever medium.

Although we have described the bony structure rather than the living flesh of musical form, the foregoing sketch of its detail will perhaps sufficiently indicate the image which must be the foundation of the idea of musical form. Since the facts of tension and motion are omnipresent in the musical substance, the dynamic aspect of this image will have appeared more striking than the static. Yet, in that retrospect which will ensue upon the completed experience of study and listening, the static facts of proportion, dimension, balance, and relation which are conspicuous in well-ordered pictorial composition emerge as vital also for the image of musical form.†

* Examples: of addition — the fifth bar of Brahms's *Rhapsody* for piano, Op. 119 (where the addition is made to appear normal by omitting in bar 4 the hitherto marked down-beat accent); of subtraction — the seven-bar period which opens Mozart's *Figaro* Overture (whose normality no one seems able to explain).

† Consider, for example, the interjection — thematically quite unrelated to the rest of the musical substance — of the phrase from the hymn, "Refresh thyself, my

That image, however, to become an idea of form, must be valued. It will be well, however, to summarize the features of that imaged object before we attempt its valuation.

Our image will comprise a substance (tone) of high sensuous appeal, organized, in part for the heightening of that appeal, but also for more intellectual interest. In this aspect, three inherent or acquired properties of the substance are significant: scaled pitch, giving impressions of measured upward and downward motion, strongly suggestive of line; variable tension (visible as qualities of activity and rest) imparting impetus and direction to the moving melodic point which "draws" that line; and harmony, creating an illusion of mass in the musical body, and vastly amplifying and diversifying the tensions already indicated, which, to the hearer whose attention is chiefly focussed on that line, seem to be concentrated in it.

This musical substance is also animated by the non-substantial factor of rhythm, subtly correlated with the tensions of the tonal substance itself, and imparting to it a sense of motion. These cohesions, resultants of tonal tension and rhythm, also often assume (doubtless from the long association of music with words) a strong similarity to the cohesions and inflections of linguistic syntax (the basic "form" of language), even though the musical substance lacks wholly the symbolic reference of words.

Our image is thus that of a substance extremely fluid, yet capable of assuming for contemplation the static aspect of design; visible also as organized through the incessant dynamic functioning of its components; and having a surface colorable appropriately to both its static and its dynamic aspects.

The valuation of this image cannot but vary with every hearer, according to his tonal sensibility and discrimination, his acuity in perceiving the static and dynamic cohesions which make for design, and his background of experience against which he must view the imaged substance. Among all these variables it would appear that no constant can be stable enough for measurement. Yet that a constant of some kind exists is proved by the general and considerably similar response of the million to the appeal of music. Sometimes, indeed, that response is so unanimous and so uni-

failing spirit," in the development section of the First Brahms symphony. This theme, immediately associable with its text, has doubtless primarily an expressive purpose. But there is also high formal value when this unexpected feature is seen against the extraordinary concentration of the musical design thus far.

form that the scientist's doubt — his chief weapon against deception — is stilled.

The response of the audience which heard our Bach concerto was an instance. That response indicated a deep delight. No small portion of that delight arose from an awareness of form. The most characteristic feature of that response was an utter stillness. Now stillness, in such ordinarily mobile creatures as men under excitement, is a very distinctive motor fact. Motor behavior is, indeed, the most immediately knowable aspect — the most direct "expression" — of emotional condition. It is in terms of motor impulse, therefore, that we may first interpret not only the valuation which that audience set upon the image of form offered them, but the valuation of that image in general.

To each factor of the whole complex image, if we take time to contemplate it, not only an intellectual identification of the factor but an emotional response to it will be aroused. The sensuous glory of musical tone, the curve of a melodic phrase, the richness and the tension of an unexpected harmony will all possess emotional interest; and to each of these — certainly if it were observed in isolation, but doubtless also when it is combined with other features — a typical motor release is appropriate. These impulses, moreover, appear only as smaller waves of motion borne upon the tide of the underlying and all-pervading rhythmic pattern — itself an illusion of motion. But in the imaginatively performed musical substance itself these details — physically, no more than tones in their varied aspects — appear, not as discrete but as related sensory entities, concrescent toward the one total impression of unified design.

Seen as a single entity, this design — comprising within itself the lesser motor suggestions we have noted — may also evoke in us an accordant, apparently single, motor impulse. The familiar motion-patterns of marching or waltzing, vividly portrayed, make it difficult for the mere listener to restrain his feet from performing (of course, on a decorous, miniature scale) those same familiar acts. But more obscurely allusive designs have also their motor implications. Our Bach concerto was such a design. It was the counterpart of no simple experience, delineable in terms of familiar motions of arms and legs. Its range of suggestion seemed far to exceed any concrete imagery — an abstraction, therefore, but drawn, nevertheless, indubitably *out of* experience. In this high abstraction the many motor impulses generated within us were held in a kind of equilibrium. And this equilibrium — no mere, inert immobility, but the exquisite balance of every motive force within us — was indeed our motor expression of delight.

That delight, however, was far greater than our account of it, stated in terms of motor response alone, makes it appear. The whole musical substance, seen as the single formed object which performance projects, had many other attributes — not the least of them sensuous — all of which combined to round out our awareness of form. Other forms will display other values, not often as high as this but comparable. We are trying to generalize and value, not the image of form offered by this concerto, but the form-image in general, and we must not lose sight of that objective.

The word form, in its simplest conversational value, means shape. Shape, however, implies pattern — a perfected shape. But the perfecting of a shape is in part an effort of selection (of the stuff to be shaped), but far more of organization. Thus a form, although it may come to rest under the contemplating eye and thus appear, in this static aspect, simply as a shape, is really an organism. An organism is — or at least was, during the process of its organization — a "living" thing whose constituent elements, functioning within the boundaries considerably determined by the selection of its substance, display what the contemplating mind recognizes as purposeful correlations. In this aspect, form appears as dynamic.

It is possible to view the tonal substance as "purely" tonal, and its organization as a product of those tensions and dispositions to motion which are perceived by any sensitive ear as inherent in that substance. In this view a perfected musical form may appear as a concrete illustration of the abstract process of organization.

Thus seen, it cannot but invite comparison with other products of organization. And particularly in contrast to the incessant jangle and disorder of the experiences of every-day life, perfect artistic form — comparable in the diversity of its contained matter to the stream of diurnal event — is order itself: order and incomparable enrichment of the sense-stimulus offered by its primary substance. The enjoyment of form thus becomes a special order of experience — an emotion whose vibration seems to course through every sentient nerve; whose motor response is a stillness even to the holding of the breath; whose consummation is the awakening of a vision of perfection. To attain to perfection in the form of a work of art is thus to offer the satisfaction of a great complex of desires — to express emotion as well as to evoke it; for to attain to perfection is to realize an ideal.

Form in Isolation

Yet neither in its static nor its dynamic aspect can form be properly viewed as a mere abstract of the process of organization. Any actual form has a substance, and the qualities of that substance, comprised in that particular form, cannot safely be ignored in the contemplation of that form. Thus any attempt to contemplate form apart from its substance — to contemplate it as the disembodied idea of organization merely — will be an abstraction *away from* reality.

Present-day criticism, observing that (as we have just seen) music does indeed present "forms in tonal motion," is largely unanimous in its verdict that it presents nothing else — that form is the essence and termination of all artistic endeavor. It cannot be denied that this idea — even when viewed in the light of our adopted definition — is legitimate. To apprehend the form of music as the organization of a purely musical substance is to form an image of purely musical experience. To value that image as purely musical is to form an idea of that experience. If, however, the image is faulty, the idea will be flawed.

Observed merely as an artistic construction, music cannot be criticized as other art-works are criticized. For in this light the third of the critical inquiries mentioned above — was the work worth doing? — must be answered wholly in terms of the constructive effort. Arts whose "substance" is more directly related to human experience are criticized (of course in varying measure) against that familiar and already valued background. To remove the background is thus to erect a new definition of art. True, to view the general experience of organization as the background against which tonal organization is to be judged is to provide a rather diaphanous background akin to that required for ordinary criticism. But a flawed background is as precarious as a flawed image; and this danger the contemporary critical attitude seems to ignore.

Yet that attitude has been widely assumed in the criticism of other arts. Students of poetic form — to take but a single example — attempt to dismiss the general background of experience in such ironical comment as "Longfellow and Whittier were full of great thoughts," and by the general advice, "It doesn't matter what you say; it is how you say it that counts." But the irony here reacts pretty severely upon the critic, for those poets, like ourselves, were only full of little thoughts about great things, and the student who dares to tell his teacher, "it doesn't matter what you say," is likely to find invoked against him a larger background of experience than linguistic structure.

49

The majesty of the verse of *Paradise Lost* is the creation of one who, considered purely as artist, was indeed a greater poet than Longfellow or Whittier. But would a profounder study of form *as organization* have made their work greater? The majesty of Milton's verse was generated, not out of primary consideration for the value of form, but out of a similarly majestic vision of human experience and its attendant perplexities — a vision dimly perceptible to a multitude of average men who find in that poem a valuable enlargement of their own narrow range.

Is it true also that the *Eroica* has something to say about heroism? If so, can that something be found within the confines of musical form, either as we have described it or as a more competent criticism would have defined it? And if that something is actually *there*, must we conclude that the *Eroica* — whether as a form or as a more comprehensive art-work — has been marred or impoverished by the inclusion of such interest? Could music, robbed of such interest, maintain its position of sisterhood with the other arts?

If that position is to be maintained, it is evident that not the form but the substance of music must be explored, in the hope of finding within that substance such a ground of relativity to the stuff of general experience as may be generally apprehended by those who have ears to hear. Quite as evidently, we shall not find that relation by exploring further the substance of music in its purely structural aspect. Rather, we must examine experience itself, as we know it, in the hope of finding some aspect of experience to which the substance and the structure of music — again as we know it — may be seen to be related.

❧ V ❧

Content in Isolation: Non-aesthetic
Idea and Emotion

Toward an ideal form, music probably rises higher than any other art. The tonal stuff of music is of great sensuous appeal; it is surely the most plastic substance ever to be molded into tangible forms; and in the creation of those forms the musician is absolved from all immediate consideration of the physical appearances and properties of *things*. The other arts deal, whether realistically or ideally, with things;* and these things, whatever their nature, the artist must somehow raise to that height of imaginative interest which will make them relevant factors in an ideal form-pattern. While all art is in no small measure abstraction, music, if only because of its unconcern with physical appearances of things, is the most fortunate of all the arts in its quest for that perfection of form which is both a delight in itself and the expression of an ideal of order.

But does music set forth no more than this ideal of order? In its dis-severance from the world of things in their physical aspect, is our art excluded from the utterance of any other than the image and the attendant feeling of form? If so, the relation of music to life is more remote than is indicated either by its history or by the high position assigned to it by musicians and their public alike. For however lofty our emotional response to form, it is certain that the emotions most important in our lives are not primarily of the aesthetic order, but are those awakened, not indeed by

---

* The "thing" represented in a supposedly abstract painting is generally — and often by a specific title — indicated by some disposition of lines or planes which, however unrepresentative of physical objects, turns out to be (like the poised squares described in the footnote on page 40) a perceptible "reality" of sensuous experience. It is unlikely that the sub-conscious (which, after all, is a nervous activity as definitely originated in and conditioned by physical experience as consciousness itself) evokes wholly abstract images.

51

mere things, but by human contacts and relations that are dependent on things. The expressive method of the other arts involves, in large measure, the representation (in varying degrees of literalness) of the concrete experiences — in the last analysis, the things — out of contact with which emotion is generated. The expressive method of music, in which the representation of things is mostly impossible, and in which even partially successful endeavor is usually repellent, must of necessity differ from that of the other arts.

Yet unless the world has been pitifully deluded, music somehow expresses not only the gratification of our desire for ideal order, but also the very tumult of human passion. The music lover has no doubt of the "reality" of this expression. He finds portrayed in music the same passions as those expressed by the other arts: the delights and the miseries of life — our immediate and personal response *to* those very things and circumstances which music is powerless to represent *as* things and circumstances. All men know these delights and these miseries, and to them, according to their sensitivity to his work, the artist expresses, more vividly than any other commmentator, the highest realities of experience. To establish expressive meaning as resident in music will therefore be to demonstrate that this art, like the others, has essential relation to non-artistic experience, and so to truth.

But how can this be? What has music to do with truth? If expression is an utterance of our awareness, whether of fact or of attendant feeling — and thus, to our apprehension, of reality itself — how can it be achieved through a substance which is the very essence of the ideal and which shrivels into insignificance the moment it is made to represent things? Here indeed is a critical dilemma. One escape — apparent rather than real, as we have already noted — is through the denial of the possibility of musical expression. The other — which we are to seek — is through the discovery of some tangible relation, more precise than the mere awareness of excitement as aroused by music, between the musical substance and the emotions born of human experience.

One of these related entities — the musical substance seen in its formal aspect — was sufficiently described in the preceding chapter, where we found the musical substance yielding an image of musical form and an attendant valuation which we may call an "aesthetic" idea. (This narrow definition of the usually far more significant term, aesthetic, is used for convenience in making the somewhat difficult distinction necessary for

52

our immediate purpose.) The larger excitement aroused by admitting into the valuation of the whole musical substance its reference to experience not of the aesthetic order — a valuation to which the aesthetic excitement will contribute incalculably — we may similarly call an experiential idea. That the two become indissolubly fused in our impression of the whole art-work is unquestioned. But the two are nevertheless distinct and essentially dissimilar entities, as was shown by the study of our illustrative stanza. That they must still be distinct and dissimilar when aroused by the far less "definitional" substance of music is evident. To explore non-aesthetic or experiential idea as it may be conveyed by music is thus our present problem.

The image of experience evoked by the so-called representative arts is an image of definable objects — of "things." Music has virtually no power of delineating things. Therefore the image of experience which must be evoked, if music is to achieve the expression of experiential idea, must have a different origin — and in all probability a different character — from that which is evoked by the direct and immediate contemplation of things. We have defined idea as an image and a valuation of experience. We have seen that that valuation is in no small part emotional. If we assume that music (as its history seems to show) has some capacity for delineating as well as merely exciting emotion, it is possible that we may find our art capable of delineating, not the image itself of experience which is an essential component of idea, but the valuation of that image. And if that valuation is vividly portrayed, it is conceivable that a plausible inference may be drawn therefrom as to the nature of the experience itself.

This, in brief, is the gist of the argument to follow. To explore emotion as a valuation-factor in idea is thus an essential preliminary to our search for, and our study of, the manner and the validity of the musical delineation of emotion.

We need hardly emphasize the importance of experiential emotion as a factor in the sterner effort as well as in the lighter joy of life. We not only play, we also work and battle and scheme and study in order that we may feel. Our labor and strife for material possession; our struggle for domination in sport or combat; our careful deploying of forces for social or political success; our patient search for the myriad dry facts whose correlation may reveal the existence of some hitherto unknown law or principle in nature — all these efforts are undertaken, hardly at all for the sake of the things, as such, upon which our effort is expended, but in order that we may feel their significance in the scheme of our personal philosophy. The value of experience may be exhibited as a kind of additive sum of its factual components; but that sum, however imposing as a mere addition, we finally measure also in terms of its ultimate emotional consequence for ourselves; and so common is this valuation that we for the most part accept emotion, or the capacity for emotion, even in notably complex and difficult problems of conduct, as the most dependable index — the "abstract and brief chronicle" — of human character. Art, accordingly, when it offers a convincing expression of emotion — convincing not merely because of its intensity, but because of its palpable origin in some high reality of experience — is justly regarded as a valid summary of the very meaning of experience. To abandon or deny the claim of music to a share in this regard is a renunciation hardly to be compensated for by an exaltation of the value of form.

In contrast to the obscure relation of music to experience, that of the representative arts is obvious. Their normal method is that of the delineation of material conditions and circumstances. If these are vividly represented we react to the delineation as if we were in the presence of reality — as if, indeed, we were protagonists in the action. We are told, for example, how Richard Feverel finds Lucy eating dew-berries — not, to be sure, that we may know merely that Richard found Lucy eating dew-berries, but that from this and the other given instances we may infer and imaginatively share the sudden submission of these two children to uncomprehended passion. What is here *described* is circumstance, not feeling; but what is here *expressed* is feeling, not circumstance. And it is certain that if Meredith had attempted to describe literally the emotions which he has here by indirection expressed, we should have responded far less generously to his suggestion. Language has, at best, a meager vocabulary of pure feeling.*

This feeling, nevertheless, is *known*. We know it, of course, chiefly as a correlative of the circumstance in which it had its origin; but we know

---

* Coleridge's famous lines:

> And slimy things did crawl with legs
> Upon the slimy sea

are as productive of repulsion as any graphic representation could be; yet there is here no word descriptive of that state of feeling. On the other hand, Goethe's highly literal expression of feeling itself:

> Es schwindelt mir, es brennt mein Eingeweide

seems, by comparison, feeble and ineffective as an expression of emotional condition.

it also as a characteristic nervous tone, appropriate to the circumstance out of which it arose, but discriminable in itself *as* nervous tone. Words, seen as mere names, are but feeble symbols for conditions of feeling. Poets, as we have seen, can endow them with more than their definitional meaning, and can so manage the very tone of verbal utterance as to make it represent the feeling appropriate to the circumstance their words portray. But if some vehicle could be found through which the characteristic tone of an emotion could be immediately portrayed, and if this utterance were precise enough so that the feeling was discriminable as the normal reaction to a particular type of experience, a considerable addition to our vocabulary, not only of feeling but of experience itself, would be acquired, and our wealth of expression enriched.

The process of expression, it is true, would be the converse of that employed by the so-called representative arts. These begin with portrayed circumstance which, as we apprehend it, generates by a kind of inference its feeling-correlative. Our proposed process begins with portrayed feeling which generates an inference of appropriate causal circumstance. But in both the result is an image and a valuation of experience.*

This reversal of the direction of what we are calling inference will be seen, in the sequel, to be an essential feature of that process of musical expression which we shall first propose as a hypothesis and then test at considerable length. The notion of reversal, if it now seems obscure, will become much clearer in the testing laboratory. But it will be well to realize now that, just as it is clear that the image of musical form, valued as we described it in the last chapter, yields the idea of musical form, so it is evident that an awareness of music as related to non-musical experience — of music as expressive — must involve an image of formed musical substance in some way recognizable as correlative to such experience. Since the literal representation of non-musical experience is all but impossible in music, this correlation can be established only through intelligible com-

---

* That both image and valuation may be faulty cannot be disputed. A sufficient illustration may be found in the numberless disasters that befall maidens who partake too generously of music as the food of love. This suggests that what exists in the shape of a mental image of experience and its valuation is often rather a "state of mind" than an "idea." That word ordinarily implies a sharpness of definition in both image and valuation, and an attendant process or activity of intellection which — as in the deplorable case just mentioned — is absent from the state of mind. The point at which idea, in the stricter sense of that word, emerges from or sinks into the mere state of mind, and the share of intellection essential to what may properly be called idea, is certainly incapable of precise definition; but it will still be difficult to discover an idea which is not an image and a valuation of experience.

munication of the feeling generally known as appropriate to experience. That feeling must be *portrayed* intelligibly to the listener — a feat which the naive music lover (collectively forming what Philip Hale once called "that noble army of music lovers who know what they like") recognizes unquestioningly as possible.* And to the extent to which feeling is portrayed, the admission becomes ineluctable that music is, like all the others, essentially a representative art.

If music is to achieve such representation, a very definite relation between the substance of music and the characteristics of experiential emotion must be shown to exist. That relation will certainly not be revealed by examination of the musical substance in the usual light of musical theory. We must study the emotion itself, and study it in the light of a possibility of the revelation we seek. Almost any of the endless experiences of life could serve as typical of the feeling we are to study; but one of the commonest, both in life and (in the estimation of the noble army) in music, will best serve our purpose.

If we take the passion of love, and consider our whole mental and emotional state while under its sway, we shall see at once that the feeling itself which makes our passion compelling is mingled with, and for its existence depends upon, a persistent awareness of the object of our feeling. For we cannot just love. We must love something or somebody; and the character of our feeling is largely determined by its object. We love men and pictures and games and puddings; but not with the same affection. Yet, although awareness of the object of our love is a vital determinant of the character of our passion, that awareness is not itself our love. There is here a mental fusion, comparable to that of form and meaning in our poetic stanza, of object and attendant feeling.

We may accordingly attempt, as in our study of the poem, to isolate the feeling-component from its objective origin and observe it for itself. If we allow our contemplation of some person or object for which we have deep and genuine affection to continue until that feeling has become live and kinetic, and then suddenly attempt to obliterate from consciousness the image of that object while retaining as fully as possible the awareness of our feeling, our mental state will appear disconcertingly simplified.

---

* I have elsewhere noted, but cannot resist the temptation to recall here, a marvelous cartoon of James Thurber's, depicting an expert in painting, high up a ladder, minutely measuring and analyzing a picture. Below, on the floor of the gallery, are two awed observers. "He knows everything about art," says one of them, "but he doesn't know what he likes!"

Our feeling, without awareness of its cause, seems far more akin to mere sensation than we supposed. Even if we are able to maintain our feeling at something like its original intensity, it will have lost enormously in definition. And again, a similar obliteration of feeling from our contemplation of its object will exhibit that object as extraordinarily reduced in interest.

It becomes evident, then, that we identify our feelings far less in terms of their intrinsic nervous tone than in terms of association with their external cause.* Yet the feeling-tone of our reaction to an object is not only an intrinsic component of our whole awareness of an object, but is a dependable index of the depth of our interest — an index which, for communication, is highly significant. For it is evident that a similar complex of experience to that which arouses a given emotion in ourselves will arouse a similar excitement in others. And it is not wholly out of loose thinking that we habitually use the word sympathy to describe our agreement with others, not merely in feeling but in thought.

We know, that is, much more about actual feeling than we are able to tell in words. Sometimes, indeed, we are able (or for full understanding are required) to make finer discriminations of feeling-tone than are ordinarily required for communication when the cause of feeling can be made clear. For there are emotions of considerable intensity for which we can find no cause in external circumstance. Such nervous conditions — probably always present in some degree, but only occasionally vivid enough to be consciously noted — we call "moods." They are aroused, either through external stimuli which have been unregistered in consciousness or have been forgotten, or through the still more obscure stimulation of the various muscular and visceral agencies which arouse emotion. Odors, sights, sounds, or contacts, whose impact is of the slightest, and also adrenal or other visceral stimulation for which no more than the obscurest physiological reasons exist, may excite remarkably vivid states of feeling — states which persistently affect our awareness of consciously noted objects. Almost always our moods have a peculiar quality of unreasonableness (particularly when they are unpleasant) which is doubtless due to the absence of any assignable cause for our feeling. Yet, unaware

* It is probably for this reason that we have contrived so feeble a vocabulary of words for the symbolization of pure feeling. It may also be for this lack of words that we have developed but a narrow mental discrimination for the intrinsic characteristics of feeling-tone. (Women, more energetically than men, may dispute the latter assertion.)

as we are of their causes, we confidently describe our moods as states of depression, ennui, willfulness, petulance, buoyancy, elation, or whatever; and it is apparent that we distinguish these states largely through the characteristic tone of the nervous conditions themselves. Our recognition is of course sharpened by the peculiar aspect given by the mood to the experience we are undergoing. If the experience is significant, we may fail to see that it is the mood which colors the experience, and not the experience which arouses the mood. It is of course seldom that our moods are vivid enough to be confused with those emotions for which experience provides a recognizable cause; but it may still be true that a persistently recurrent mood, although confidently assumed to be a quality of the experiences it has colored, will become crystallized into a personal characteristic which our friends will interpret as a part of our "disposition."

Specific feeling-tone, the more sharply noted in our moods because we cannot identify it otherwise than in terms of feeling, is of course characteristic also of our experiential emotions. For many such states — doubtless because their experiential origin is perceptible — we have indeed invented verbal symbols, some of which seem to imply feeling primarily, while others suggest experiential condition rather than feeling. Even those words, however, which symbolize feeling chiefly will be found to imply at the same time a general experiential condition in relation to which alone the implied feeling is imaginable. (Note that there is here an instance of that inference of causal circumstance from expressed feeling which we have already mentioned, and will find more fully illustrated, as a factor in the process of musical expression.) Such words as awe and sublimity, doubt and faith, agony, frustration, misery, or delight, if sufficiently pondered, will awaken in us not only images of feeling, different in each case but at least as identifiable in terms of feeling-tone as the causeless moods just considered; and each will also imply an appropriate region of knowable experience within which such feeling will normally arise. Doubt and faith, of course, may be felt in such various contexts as religion or love or politics, and the feeling will vary with the context although, with the barest hint of it, that context may be vividly inferred from the word alone. Awe and sublimity, on the other hand, arise out of less variable experience and yield somewhat more definite inferences of experience. But the awareness of experience they arouse is a feeble counterpart indeed of the intensity with which we should respond to a true and vivid portrayal of those feelings.

58

Content in Isolation

Not only our moods, then, but the emotions born of external experience also, have their characteristic nervous tone. We *know* these feeling-tones because they are the correlatives of experience as we undergo it, and constitute no small part of our valuation of the images of fact offered by external experience. Words, which are symbols for things and acts, their qualities, and the relations between them, portray facts of experience with such vividness that an attendant feeling cannot fail to be aroused. Only by indirection, however, do words effectively portray feeling. And if we can achieve, through music, a revelation more direct or more exact or more intense or more true of the feeling which Keats desires us to undergo when, as he tells us of himself:

> . . . on the shore
> Of the wide world I stand alone and think,
> Till love and fame to nothingness do sink.

then indeed we shall have given larger boundary to the effective language of experience. Delineation of the tone of such excitement, which we shall try to demonstrate is possible through music, will contribute largely to this language.

Strictly speaking, this nervous excitement *is* the emotion. By no means, however, is it the whole, or even the most clearly knowable characteristic of that state of excitement connoted by our ordinary use of the word emotion. The psychologist will recognize in that state three essential factors. The first, naturally, is our awareness of the stimulus — the experience, usually external, which arouses the excitement. The nervous tension which results is the second — that tension with which we have just dealt. But there is a third factor — as definitely felt as the nervous tension itself, but more definitely knowable because it may be externally perceived — the motor outlet of the excitement.

The term "kinaesthetic," implying "felt movement" — movement sensed, that is, both as impulse and act — has been invented to describe the combined nervous impulse and motor outlet we are observing. The impulse may vent itself directly and involuntarily and still be recognized, either by the subject himself or by an observer, as the appropriate muscular "expression" of the impulse. But it also may be, and often is, inhibited.* Inhibition, however, does not imply complete destruction of the

* Dewey's theory that "affective phenomena" — emotions as apart from mere sensations — arise only "when the tendency awakened undergoes inhibition," should perhaps receive more attention than is given it in the text. But the nature, rather than

original motor impulse, but rather its re-direction. When a motor impulse is thus inhibited, another than the immediate or "natural" motor response occurs; but some sort of motor act is inevitable as a result of emotional excitement. The motor impulse, when it is thus inhibited and re-directed, is *felt*. It is indeed the actual evidence of our feeling-state; for the state of nervous tension is not perceptible in the excited nerves themselves. And it is this feeling which differentiates and gives character to our emotional states. But whether they are immediate or re-directed, we recognize motor responses as definitely characteristic of the mental states that generate them, and we thus naturally regard our motor outlets as, in the most literal sense, the "expression" of our feeling. This third factor of the whole emotional experience, like the second, may prove to have important musical correlatives, and must be observed more closely.

Some motor response to emotion is inevitable. Fortunately, however, for our social life, much of this outlet takes place through muscles which for other practical reasons are consciously controllable. In the infant, who has not yet learned conscious control, every sensation of pleasure or pain is accompanied by prodigious vocal and muscular demonstration. As we grow older, we cease to kick and scream at every disappointment; but our behavior when under the influence of stimulants or narcotics, or in partial anaesthesia, shows that we have not destroyed but have only inhibited these original impulses. We learn to smile sweetly (or perhaps a little sourly) when we would rather scowl; to vent our anger in words or looks when we would rather strike. But this re-direction of our impulses by no means renders them invalid as indications of our real emotion. It produces, indeed, a kind of socialization of our motor behavior which, while perhaps reducing its physical effectiveness, renders it even more intelligible as an index of feeling.

It is needless to discuss in detail the more usual motor acts which are thus commonly understood. Gait, gesture, facial "expression," and that most subtle release which is apparent in verbal inflection — all these, as indices of feeling, are consistently taken into account, along with more intellectual verbal communications, as important conveyors of meaning in our every-day intercourse. Our motor behavior may intensify our words, or it may so effectively belie them that we are seen, not merely to

the precise origin of the emotional excitement is our problem, and sufficient attention seems to us to be given to the results of inhibition so that the minuter question need not be raised.

be attempting to deceive our friends, but actually to be deceiving ourselves.

In addition to these familiar types of motor expression, more obscure impulses exist which apparently have not been, and perhaps cannot be, effectively studied. Inhibited motor impulse of course results in curtailed muscular execution; but inhibition does not lessen, but may even increase our *desire* for its execution.

We do not physically embrace the beautiful stranger whom we encounter in the street; but our imagination is uninhibited. Nor is it only in those situations where propriety forbids their execution that ineffectual motor impulses arise. They are also possible where we lack the physical equipment for their execution. It is not only in dreams that we sprout wings and fly. When we are in the full flush of excitement due to some unexpected or greatly desired success, we say that we are *elated* — that we are borne up off the earth. That word, invented long before anybody but Daedalus had succeeded in flying, gives clear etymological evidence of the type of impulse we are describing. The number of words immediately definitional of such impulse is perhaps not large, for the impulse itself (as in the case just mentioned) is only a part of our whole awareness, and is thus too faint or too obscure to demand precise verbal symbolization. Yet verbal evidence of such impulse is not hard to find. There is no muscular agency which can cause "each particular hair to stand an-end" in human beings; but they can all feel horror, which, literally, is bristling. Similarly, ecstasy is being outside oneself; rapture and transport signify various fashions of being "carried away"; depression is being weighed down by some intolerable burden of the spirit, and hence, also, a spiritual fashion of moving under that burden. And even the college sophomore, not long ago, invented for a condition of imagined motor response to a variety of stimuli (often, it is true, sophomoric) the vivid phrase, "that sends me."

Here the motor impulse, ineffectual though it be, is definite enough to be characterized verbally; but there are doubtless a good many impulses of this order (whether less vivid or merely less frequent) which have never been named but are nevertheless a part of our total consciousness of emotion. If these lesser impulses were to be defined or somehow represented intelligibly, we should recognize them — as we recognize not merely transient emotion but the whole nature of a man's past emotional experience in the character (which is literally the engraving) of his facial expression —

as realities of experience. And to discover such utterance would be, again, to add incalculably to the effective vocabulary of experience.

Our cognitions of external fact, then, are amplified and made personal to ourselves — and others — through endless complexities of nervous tension and motor impulse. The bond between knowing and feeling is close — so close that not only does external experience, clearly defined, serve as a sign of the feeling proper to such experience: manifestations of feeling, also, if insufficiently definite, serve as signs of the general or usual cause or origin of the displayed feeling. We *know* our feelings — know them almost more intimately than we know the experiences that arouse them. We communicate them, in words, only circuitously; for words symbolize most clearly the facts of experience rather than the emotions that result from experience, so that the direct and immediate utterance of feeling is but an impeded avenue of expression for language. We supplement language, accordingly, through such accessories of utterance — facial expression, gesture, gait, verbal inflection (and in some cases by inflection almost devoid of verbal meaning, such as the mere "Oh!" of Henry James's Lord Mark) — which are taken by everybody as signs, not of feeling merely, but also of the condition responsible for such feeling.

Is it improbable that music — which fails as completely as does a bitterly compressed lip to indicate the external causes of bitterness — may likewise suggest the nervous strains and the muscular contractions that characterize bitterness? Can it represent the familiar characteristics of feeling with such clarity that not only can the feeling be recognized as familiar, but the sort of experience that generated it may with some certainty be inferred? Is not this sort of inference a common and dependable contribution to our understanding of experience?

The noble army of music lovers answers this question without hesitation affirmatively. That army, also, is not the ignorant mob contemned by the learned. It has shown a collective force which, if it has not wholly determined the course of the history of our art, has at least compelled the creators of it to pursue lines of endeavor which the army can follow. Indeed, unless music possessed the power of expression its history would be found in Hoyle.

If it is an expressive art, there must be a method of expression — a method rooted not in the exceptional sensitivity of the artist but in that simpler consciousness of tonal relations which the million possess, and can cultivate. The elemental processes underlying such a method should not be sought in the obscure and difficult mechanics of tonal organization as such, but rather in some perceptible relation of tones and rhythms to the mechanics of thought and feeling which everybody knows and pursues.

We should be ready, after this long preliminary examination of these things, to search for the elements of musical expression.

❦ *VI* ❧

The Two Elements of Musical Expression

H AVING now defined the field of experience to which the musical substance as a vehicle of expression must relate, our next task must be to discover, first, the factors of that substance which may function for expression, and secondly, the manner in which they achieve that end.

We have seen that each of the three elements of musical structure contributes to the fact of musical form. They function toward that end through the operation of two "activities" — those of tonal tension and motion. But tension and motion are also conspicuous features of many other operations than that exhibited in the behavior of the musical substance. Within that substance, both motion and tension do function for the establishment of syntactical cohesion; but even there, as we saw at the outset of our study, each of these bore reference to fields of experience quite extraneous to musical form, and it was with some difficulty that, in our discussion of form, we restricted their implications to that field. Although they were indubitably characteristic of the behavior of the musical substance, they might also be transferred to, and thus appear characteristic of, the behavior of quite another and perhaps a more palpable body.*

That more palpable body may indeed be the human body, whose actual

---

* Program music — the worst as well as the best of it — is the product of such a transfer. Sometimes the transfer is made, not by the composer but by the hearer. It was patently the ground of that indolent-minded imagery which turned Rellstab's innocent babbling about moonlight on the Lake of Lucerne into the familiar but utterly misleading title for Beethoven's C♯-minor piano sonata — one of the first thoroughly introspective and one of the most profoundly depressed pieces in musical literature. But it is also the basis of that sort of musical imagery which created his Pastoral Symphony. Here, to be sure, the tensions and motions portrayed are not those of the country itself where the listener is supposed to be arriving, but those of his mind as he arrives. It would be quite gratuitous to imagine (for example) the fermata at the fourth bar as a pause for delighted contemplation of the pastoral scene; but it would be equally uncalled-for to regard as meaningless Beethoven's superscription for the movement (*Erwachen heiterer Empfindungen bey der Ankunft auf dem Lande*). What he portrays *is* feeling; but it is not feeling in the ab-

64

propellant is the mind in action. For as we have seen, emotion — one of the behavior-patterns of a mind in action — involves a complex of nervous tensions and their attendant motor releases. That complex is of course submerged in our larger total consciousness — an awareness cognizant of both the cause and the implications of our excitement. Yet that excitement is resolvable into facts of tension and motor-impulse; and these, in their common manifestation, serve as "signs" of our total mental activity, appropriate to and characteristic of the activity itself. (Laughter, for example, has a thousand possible inflections, often indicative, far more than the words which mostly generate it, of emotional attitudes ranging from spontaneous gaiety to bitter irony.)

If, then, we continue to define expression as the intelligible utterance and communication of a mental state, our immediate problem will take this form: Can the musical composer so select and manipulate tonal motions and tensions that, in addition to the image of musical form, they may yield the image of a mind under excitement? And may he thus portray, not merely excitement in general, but that particular excitement which is our characteristic response to a particular complex of exciting circumstances? If so, these tonal motions and tensions may prove to be the elements of musical expression.

Any private soldier in the noble army of music lovers will give an affirmative answer. He has no difficulty in distinguishing a dirge from a dance, nor in associating each of these pieces with some extramusical experience to which it is appropriate. Yet if you ask even an officer in that army — corporal or general, according to his musical experience — *how* he distinguishes them, he will hesitate. If you persist in your demand, he will come up with some such answer as that the dirge drags its feet while the dance capers. He is quite right, and he shows a more active imagination than the purist who asserts that these capers are no more than the characteristics of a *tönend bewegte Form.* For his naive answer really recognizes that motions and tensions in the music are what make it appropriate to the mood of the dirge or of the dance.

stract. It is the feeling of one who breathes country air and senses therewith a thousand similar but unnameable contributions to well-being. And it should not be forgotten than many by no means naive listeners, in the earlier 18th century, *expected* musical motion to evoke an image of physical motion. Bach, for example, in approaching the central Christian mystery (*Et incarnatus est*) in the B-minor Mass, portrays the descent of the Holy Ghost (*qui propter nos et nostram salutem descendit de coelis*) not only by an unexpected and most suggestive modulation, but quite literally by quietly descending arpeggios in the violins.

Not all music, of course, is as directly indicative as are these pieces of the types of experience that can be denoted by motion and tension. Hence, as we ponder our question, How?, it ramifies uncomfortably. The elements of music, we have always been taught, are melody, harmony, and rhythm. Observed exclusively as constituents of musical form, their only function will appear to be that of structure, and they will possess none of that extramusical reference which is essential to expression as we are conceiving it. These structural elements do indeed generate motions and tensions such as we are now concerned with; but tension and motion, in so far as they provide the tonal cohesions essential to form, are functional attributes, not the real elements, of the formed musical substance.

Our simple query, then — which is indeed an attempt to justify analytically the intuition of the noble army — will take this form: How can tension and motion be transferred from their status as agents, not elements, of formal structure, to the status of elements, not agents, of musical expression? As elements of expression, how do they function? And can that function be so far extended as to warrant our assumption that music is an *intelligibly* expressive art? To answer these questions we shall find it necessary to examine individually the expressive implications of both tension and motion. But certain more general questions must precede that inquiry.*

Through this transfer from the status of structural agent to that of expressive element, a great increment of meaning is to be added to that value of syntactical cohesion which motion and tension contribute to the formal structure of music. This increment may thus appear analogous to that which we found added to words through the agency of poetic structure. But this analogy will prove false. We found the poetic increment of meaning to be, in the last analysis, definitional — of the same order, that is, as the primary and intrinsic symbolic meaning resident in the unpoetized word. But what must here accrue, if tension and motion are to become elemental for expression, is an increment of a different order: not a widening of their intrinsic syntactical force, but the acquisition of another sort of meaning — one which these factors, in their formal aspect, did not

* It is perhaps needful to note here that all these questions relate to the matter of the expressed idea, and not to the manner (also rightly called expressive) of its utterance. Obviously, the manner of an utterance must be chosen for its fitness to the matter, and it can hardly be chosen until the matter is understood. The devices comprised in the performer's technique of expression will be discussed in the following chapter, in their proper light as secondary factors or agents of expression.

possess at all. (It was on this ground that Professor Pratt's distinction between formal and expressive form had to be rejected.)

Quite evidently we shall not find the clue to this transfer of status by further examination of tension and motion in their formal aspect. As elements of expression they must assume a function of portrayal; and their fitness for that function will be more readily discovered by a study of the thing to be portrayed than by theoretical inquiry into abstract possibilities of portrayal resident in tension and motion. That "thing" is an image of non-musical experience; and such an image, if music is really to prove expressive, it must in some way intelligibly evoke.

We saw in the last chapter that an emotional experience normally involves three factors: first, the awareness of an exciting stimulus (ordinarily but not necessarily external to the recipient); secondly, a characteristic nervous excitement (describable as tension, but of vastly greater variety than that word immediately connotes); and thirdly a motor outlet, usually in some degree inhibited, of this tension. These factors are so generally present in emotional states that it is allowable to speak of them as the elements of emotional experience.

Our mental images of emotional experience are reducible to these elements. Our problem, then, is to discover what features of these images are portrayable by music, and to discern the manner or process by which that portrayal is achieved.

Two of those factors of experience, nervous excitement and motor release, are themselves manifestations of tension and motion. The musical substance exhibits tension and motion as features of its structure. Thus the first of those questions we asked a moment ago — How can these attributes of the musical substance become elemental for musical expression? — will appear quite simple. Tension and motion can become elemental for expression if they are designed, not merely to effect the cohesions essential to form, but also to *represent* familiar characteristics of feeling.*

Two "objects," then — two primary characteristics of feeling — are to be portrayed: the nervous tension aroused by the stimulus and the mo-

---

* This word "represent" will deeply alarm the music lover if he takes it as implying the representation of external physical fact (the first of the usual elements of emotional experience) after the manner of the other arts. But he should reflect that the portrayal of physical fact, however realistic, is not the real objective of art in any medium. That objective is to evoke an image of experience of a very unusual kind — one which, since it is also intended to awaken the sense of beauty, is much

tor impulse consequent upon the tension. If we take these in their order, our first inquiry will be: How far, and through what precise agencies within its substance, is music capable of portraying the familiar nervous tensions of emotion?

THE ELEMENT OF TONE-STRESS

Anyone who has the least familiarity with music will see that its whole substance, whether of tone or rhythm, appears in a constant and essential condition of varied stress. Indeed, in the variety, sublety, and range of intensity of its stress-suggestions, music is incomparable. The curve of verbal syntax, as we have seen, can compel a high degree of suspense; verbal rhythm, whether in poetry or prose, gives a vivifying suggestion of motive force and action; the sound-values of words, approaching onomatopoeia, may cause the audible surface of verbal utterance to intensify incalculably the concurrent interest not only of syntactical structure but of definitional meaning. But the musical counterparts of these things are far more compelling. The curve of melody, regarded merely as curve, floats at an altitude which verbal syntax can seldom attain; musical rhythm is incomparably more vital than verbal rhythm; and verbal inflection can hardly reach even the lower level of sensuous appeal inherent in musical tone. The painter, again, has at his command color stresses ranging from the most harmonious to the most discordant; but his "utterance" of these is inevitably static, so that within the same frame he can hardly progress (as in successive episodes the poet or the musician may progress) from calm to violence.

An extensive correlation between tonal stress and nervous tension thus appears plausible. But before this correlation can be said to identify tonal stress as an element of musical expression, many detailed questions must be answered. Where, precisely, in the musical substance does the sugges-

more than an image of factual event. Indeed, the total image of experience may often be vivid and compelling in almost inverse proportion to the literalness of the portrayal of factual circumstance. The abstractionists in both music and painting are certainly right in their endeavor to lift their work far above the level of mere factual representation. Yet the effort of the really imaginative abstract painter is probably no different in essence from the effort of any really imaginative conventional artist. Both strive to evoke the *feeling* of the given experience. The word feeling is such a common symbol for superficial excitement that it is a most deceptive equivalent for that comprehensive awareness of experience of which we are now thinking. In reality, the "appreciation" of art requires an arousing of this awareness. Nobody seems to speak of the "appreciation" of experience; yet precisely that is requisite for the appreciation of any art.

tion of stress reside? Is it merely tonal, or do other factors of the substance contribute to the suggestion? Is it measurable, either as to its intensity or its character? And, if it is a composite suggestion, how do the components function for the portrayal of what may be felt as a single state of nervous tension, characteristic of our emotional attitude toward a given experience? How, that is, shall we identify as a unit that complex of musical functions which is to serve as a single element of expression? For an element must somehow appear as a unit.

We can hardly answer these questions in their given order, but they will be dealt with somehow, either here or in the sequel. Since they will require further observation of the musical substance, whose structure we have already examined, repetition will be to some extent inevitable, but the new light in which the facts are observed may in some measure relieve the tedium.*

The musical portrayal of our awareness of nervous tension is composite. It is conveyed chiefly through tonal tension, but also through rhythm.

Three types of tone-relation suggest stress. Two of these appear in melody, one in harmony. The simplest stress-relation is that of relative height and depth in pitch. Progressions from low tones to high (or more precisely from grave to acute, since the terms low and high are really figurative) are generally felt as ascending spatially. Ascent performed by the human body is usually laborious. Thus an upward-tending tone-series, unless complicated by other factors, will almost invariably suggest increasing effort, while a downward series has the opposite value. Although this association is quite primitive in its simplicity, it is exemplified in a vast majority of musical progressions to climax and anticlimax; and if the moving musical substance is not merely a line but a harmonic mass, the sense of strain may be vastly augmented. Contrary motion between a descending bass and a rising melodic line will further heighten the tension, since it widens the apparent distance between the rising melodic line and its foundation.

* Almost every item we shall consider has long been the object of minute physical or psychological investigation. We have no space even for a bare summary of these studies, but our statements, we believe, will be in accord with the soundest of them. A clear and comprehensive summary will be found in Leonard Meyer's *Emotion and Meaning in Music*, already cited. That title may appear to imply an investigation of the same problem we are studying; but he is chiefly concerned with the minute examination of structure and our emotional reactions to structure. In so far as he speaks of the extramusical suggestion of music, he at least appears not to contradict our general contention. Whether he would approve our solution is another question.

To this primary but persistent value of spatial and gravitational stress in pitch relations, a far more potent and diversified suggestion of tension was added when harmony was discovered. For it not only provided the contrasts of consonance and dissonance, but finally established a new view of scalar tone-relation which was to be fundamental to musical structure for three hundred years. Tonality, that is, supplanted modality. We have already seen how tonality establishes an ineluctable, quasi-gravitational relation, not only of melodic tones but of supporting harmonic tones as well, to an incessantly implied (but not always consciously noted) tonic or key-note.

In our discussion of form, we described the nature of the tonic and its function in the ordered scheme of musical syntax. But this same tonic, now seen as governing a texture whose tensions and motions may portray those of emotion, acquires an unexpected increment of meaning, not only contributory to heightened interest in form, but also elemental for expression. We have already noted that, in the perspective of form, the successive tones of melody, perceived in their relation to the tonic, are discriminable as rest tones and active tones; that the rest tones are the notes of the tonic chord in the momentarily governing key; and that all the other notes of the scale, whether diatonic or chromatic, are active. These tend, in melody, to progress to the nearest rest tone. They may, however, make considerable excursions before reaching that goal; they may indeed never reach it, being deflected from their original orbit by some other attractive center; but the tendency is nevertheless observable in "good" melody. (Note, however, that they *tend* to *move* — that there are here *simultaneous* implications of both tension and motion.) These unmistakable impressions of tonal rest and activity, clearly evident in melody, are significant certainly for form. How they may also function for expression will be seen when we come to examine that process in detail. The possibility, not the operation, of that function is our immediate problem.

Rest and activity are evident also, in a still more complex and suggestive aspect, in the harmonic relations of consonance and dissonance. Consonance (or concord — the musician uses these words as synonyms) implies tonal, but not necessarily syntactical, rest. Dissonance implies unrest merely, for discord may be sensuously pleasing. But these values, patently similar to rest and activity in melody, offer endless modifications of melodic tension.

There are only two completely consonant *harmonies* — the major and minor triads. Consonant *intervals* are much more numerous — the unison, the perfect fifth and octave and, in certain conditions, the perfect fourth, together with the major and minor thirds and sixths; but while these, in their simple form, usually imply one or another of the consonant harmonies, they lose their consonant implication when combined with other intervals to form dissonant combinations. The inherent, but still inexplicable, suggestions of brightness or joy in the major triad, and of pain or darkness in the minor, although far more evident to the ears of Mozart's day than to our own, still possess positive expressive value.

There are, even in classical harmony, almost innumerable dissonances, of all degrees of harshness. If a dissonant chord be examined in isolation, its harshness will appear to depend on the number and the character of the contained dissonant intervals. The harshest of these is the minor second (as B up to C) with its inversion, the major seventh (C up to B). The softest are the minor seventh (C up to B♭) with its inversion (B♭ up to C), and the diminished fifth (B up to F). Yet the diminished fifth is the audible equivalent of the augmented fourth (B up to E♯) which, because these tones are now heard in the perspective of a different tonic, is often quite harsh. Similarly, the augmented fifth (C up to G♯) is distinctly harsh, although it is the audible equivalent of the consonant minor sixth (C up to A♭). Harshness, in any case, is more relative than intrinsic, for a comparatively smooth discord may appear as very poignant if it occurs within a considerable area of concord, while a comparatively harsh discord, surrounded by still harsher combinations, will seem grateful.*

It is needless to describe in greater detail the structure and the intrinsic tensions of harmonic combinations. In the vast preponderance of extant musical literature — that in which both the purpose and the achievement of expression are most conspicuous — it is evident that tonality provides a center of convergence for the cohesive forces of both melodic and harmonic structure.†

---

* During the nineteenth century, pure concord became almost obsolete, and classical chord-structure in superposed thirds was largely abandoned early in the twentieth. The distinction between concord and discord has thus been supplanted by a discrimination between softer and harsher tone-combinations. The older harmonic logic, dependent on a "visible" tonic, has thus become blurred. Linear counterpoint is largely unconcerned with harshness; but harshness is still a considerable factor in the listener's interest, and it may still be approximately accounted for in the number and the disposition of simultaneously heard half-steps (minor seconds) and their inversions.

† This is apparently as true of contemporary music as of the older, generally

Tonality also provides the center of convergence for those tensions which we are trying to exhibit as basic for musical expression. Thus there is no intrinsic difference between a tension which functions for design and one which functions for expression. But there is a great difference between an expressive design and one which, although its tensions possess every essential for syntactical coherence, still "says" nothing. For a design, to be expressive, must somehow bear reference to extramusical experience, and its expressiveness (unless the word expressive is itself re-defined) will be determinable accordingly. We can offer no criteria for such judgment until our hypothesis has been fully set forth. At the moment, we are only trying to demonstrate the existence of a vast resource for musical expression. But we have said enough to make it apparent that a given tonal tendency, structurally disallowed,* will heighten or otherwise alter the tension of the passage in which it occurs; that, for example, an extreme harmonic tension, suddenly resolving into smoothness, may convey more than a merely structural sense of release; and that a thousand unsuspected behaviors of the tonal substance may be found which will not merely enhance the interest of the structure but may immediately suggest a type of feeling knowable as that which characterizes our normal response to extramusical experience.

We have emphasized the fact of tonal tension without particularly noting the motion which is implied in, and is also the normal outcome or product of, tension. That is because we shall examine in a moment the far more obvious rhythmic motion of the musical body, to whose significance the motor implication inherent in tension will strongly contribute. Our immediate search, indeed, has been for a possible musical correlative or counterpart of that nervous tension which we have seen to be elemental in emotional experience. It was needful to define as clearly as possible this correlative, since the fact itself of nervous tension is highly characteristic of that image of emotional experience which music, if it is to prove ex-

familiar art. Indeed, the notion of atonality, envisioned during the 'teens and 'twenties of this century as an emancipation from outworn practice, is now almost universally abandoned as chimerical. It is of course true that tonality, in contemporary practice, has been vastly expanded in range and correspondingly attenuated as a "visible" cohesive force; the new procedure has extensively re-defined the term; but tonality is still the underlying principle of musical cohesion — which is to say, of musical intelligibility.

* The analogy seems significant between "disallowed" tonal tension and inhibited (and thus re-directed) motor impulse in the human nervous organism.

pressive, must evoke. But we also recognize motor impulse as inherent in tension, and shall by no means ignore its importance.

Ample illustration will be offered when we come to test the validity of our whole hypothesis of musical expression. But enough has been said to justify the assumption that in the fact of tonal tension, together with the implications of motion inherent in it, we have found that correlative and representative of elemental nervous tension which we have been seeking, and that we have therefore identified an actual *element of musical expression*.

This assumption will soon be elaborately tested. In the discussion incidental thereto a single verbal symbol for this element will obviously be needful. A term which implies not only the tension itself but the motor implication inherent in it would be desirable. An imposing (and forbidding) derivative from the Greek might possibly have been concocted. Lacking that invention, we have chosen the term *tone-stress* which we shall use under the assumption that inherent motor implication is to be understood as included in its meaning.

THE ELEMENT OF IDEAL MOTION

Our first element of expression is the correlative of an element of emotional experience — nervous tension. Another element of such experience is generally recognized — the motor outlet of tension. The direction of our search for a second element of expression is thus unmistakably indicated. It should be the musical correlative of our familiar motor impulses and motor acts when under the strain of emotion.

The structural element, rhythm, will at once suggest itself as the correlative we are seeking. But the structural implication of that term is far from adequate as a suggestion of the whole motor aspect of music when seen as a moving tonal mass. It suggests merely the behavior of that mass, whereas what we are seeking is the correlative of a human body animated by an excited mind. The deficiency of the term for our purpose will be apparent from a moment's study.

In its simplest manifestation, musical rhythm is definable as the symmetrical (but not necessarily mathematical) disposition, in time, of moments, partly of tonal, but mostly of dynamic stress and non-stress (accent). As far as it goes, this description is applicable to poetic meter; and in consequence the conventional symbols for that meter are often used as a graph of musical rhythm. The accompanying scheme will serve as a

73

−◡ ◡|− −|−◡ ◡|− − |− ◡◡|− −|− ◡◡|−

graph of the rhythmic *pattern* of the opening of the *Allegretto* of Beethoven's Seventh symphony. But no one familiar with the music would accept the graph as an adequate indication of the motor sense engendered in us by the music itself. Much would have to be added to make it a true symbol for the image of motion projected even by the simple structure of the first twenty-four bars. For although the unstable 6/4 chord which precedes this theme has no apparent motion, its harmonic instability has something of that significance offered by the inverted question-mark at the beginning of interrogative sentences in Spanish; and the implication of this interrogative opening should properly affect our sense of the ensuing thought (and indeed of the whole piece, since the same chord closes the movement). And when the violas and 'celli add their grave, sinuous line of melody to this same rhythmic structure, our motor awareness of the original pattern becomes vastly expanded. It is evident that our total mental impression of motor impulse may be highly complex, and that its musical correlative, to become an adequate portrayal of that motion, must borrow from all the structural elements of music.

Even the characteristics of the bare tonal substance, apart from its organization, may contribute to the conveyed motion-suggestion. We might have added to the graph some indication of the varied tonal intensities (by no means mechanically similar in successive rhythmic units) of the accents and non-accents of the pattern. This would have imparted a little more of the actual motion impulse conveyed by the music. But we could have devised no graph for the timbre of the low-registered strings which so appropriately continue the interrogative hint given by the winds in the 6/4 chord. (Imagine the theme itself in the winds!) This timbre, of course, has no intrinsic motor-suggestion; but, in this low register, it imparts to the musical body a kind of elasticity (which *is* a characteristic of motion) and thus gives a sense of strangeness to this gravely moving "thing."

Leaving now our illustration and speaking more generally, we may see that both melody and harmony, while still observed in their structural aspect, may conjoin with rhythm to heighten the portrayal of motion. Ascent and descent in pitch, already noted as significant for tension, are equally important for motor suggestion. For not only has a melodic line an upward or downward direction. Its progress may be continuous (in "conjunct" scale-wise steps) or discontinuous (in leaping intervals);

74

and in either case these steps may be smooth (legato) or detached (staccato), and may show an infinity of gradations in energy. If all this could be indicated graphically, our bare rhythm-outline for the Beethoven theme would be filled in at every instant *between* the marked moments of accent or non-accent, and would indicate no longer a mere pattern but a reality of motion.

Nor is this all. Dynamic emphasis, additional to that required for the definition of the basic meter, may suggest distinctive characteristics of physical or nervous energy; and all these features, conjoined with the intrinsic motor-impulses of consonant or dissonant harmony, may embody the depicted motion in an apparently corporeal musical mass whose weight and volume may be adjusted (as, for instance, no dancer's body could be adjusted) to the portrayal, not merely of motion but of the vital impulse to motion activating a sentient being.

Here, then, it is not too much to say that we find a clear correlative of that motor impulse which is an elemental factor in emotional experience. Accordingly, it seems justifiable to regard this musical equivalent of motor impulse and activity as a second *element of musical expression*.

How far-reaching may be the implications of musically portrayed tension and motion can be indicated only when we come to test the hypothesis of expression which is now, in its elemental factors, nearly complete. A suitable verbal identification of this second element also will then be needful. We found the term "tone-stress" inadequate for our first element because it fails to imply the motion-impulse inherent in tonal tension. The apparently obvious term, "rhythm," for our second element, is no more satisfactory, for it fails altogether to imply those intimations of tension which remain evident in the musical substance, even when that tension has assumed the guise of motion. Lacking again the verbal invention which would yield a fully appropriate term, we have borrowed a phrase from Edmund Gurney — one which we use, however, in a considerably different sense from his — and shall call our musical correlative of psychological motor impulse *ideal motion*.

Is our search for the actual elements of musical expression ended? To us, it appears so, and for the following reasons:

The two elements of expression we have described and tentatively identified are contrived, out of the original structural substance of music, through an effort which, although it must be largely structural in aim, may also be an effort at portrayal. In this effort, we have found all the structural factors of music utilizable. But in their aspect as agents for portrayal, these elements may be seen as the palpable correlatives of two similarly elemental factors in the psychological experience of emotion. Since the musical substance is patently unsuited to the portrayal of that extramusical stimulus which is ordinarily the first and originative factor in emotional experience, there are no other psychological factors to be portrayed. Our hypothetical elements have employed and exhausted the apparent resources of the structural substance for portrayal; and if we were right in basing our search for the elements of expression on a study of the thing to be expressed, and on the fitness of the vehicle for expression, no other truly elemental factors may be expected to be revealed.

We have thus established the basis of our further inquiry. But even with our elements identified, their full import has by no means been suggested. For the sake of analytical clarity we have exhibited tone-stress and ideal motion separately, and thus as considerably independent of each other. But in the actual musical substance these elements are not the separate and discrete entities we have described. Intimations of tension are offered simultaneously with intimations of motion; they must be simultaneously apprehended; and they must be interpreted as correlative intimations toward an awareness which, once it is formed, is perhaps hardly cognizant of the facts of tension and motion which evoked it. Analytically, this concrescence of diverse intimations makes for difficulties in the identification of the component suggestions. Synthetically (i.e., in normal listening, unencumbered by analytical effort) it contributes vastly to the vividness of expressive suggestion. For if a portrayed tension is perceptibly cognate to a simultaneously conveyed motor suggestion, the one will incalculably augment the other.

On the other hand, since tonal tension and rhythm are the basic features of any tonal fabric, the primary suggestions offered by our elements of expression cannot but appear in any and every intelligible tonal fabric. Like the intimations often conveyed by words, these may be of no interest. Since they are also, in substance, identical with those cohesive forces which yield the impression of syntactical order, they may appear to offer no more than the interest of structure. Even so, that interest may be high, and in a very real sense expressive, for in the more restricted area of structure they still offer an actual image of experience — the experience of perfect order, whose valuation is significant.

The Two Elements of Musical Expression

But those same tensions and motions which may thus be used, as many think, abstractly, characterize also the feeling states aroused by external experience. (The idea of perfect order in music would be far less compelling if it were not also an idea derivable from wholly non-musical experience.) And should the creative composer's musical design (itself perfectly ordered) appear as also characteristic of the feeling aroused by significant non-musical experience, the interest of that design can hardly fail to be widened. For feeling will now not only be directly excited. It will be *portrayed*; and an image of external experience to which this portrayed feeling is appropriate may be formed — an image derived, not from the portrayal of the exciting fact of experience which is the usual source or origin of our feeling, but from the feeling itself which, as a part of our valuation of experience, is as much a part of our whole idea as is the image, or the direct awareness, of the circumstance. (That awareness is itself a mental image.) An obvious instance may be adduced.

The simple image of marching which our humble soldier in the army of music lovers so readily formed was an image of extramusical experience. A musical-minded hearer who failed to form such an image during a performance of the third movement of Tchaikovsky's *Pathétique* symphony would be an object of wonder to his fellows. Even these more sentient hearers, however, might well feel the behavior suggested by the motions and tensions of that music to be beyond enactment by their physical limbs. But that very inhibition might well expand the simple image of marching into a sense of exhilaration rooted in far more complex experience than could be compacted into the "utterance" of tramping feet. Imaginary feet, equal to that utterance, might however be evoked, impelled to their more adequate utterance by imagined tensions and motions implied by those same qualities in the musical substance.

We commented, in the preceding chapter, on feeling as being ordinarily derived from our awareness of confronted circumstance, and on the method of the representative arts as being in accord with that usual order. They represent, and thus arouse a mental image of, external experience; our response to that representation is in large part a feeling-state, derived therefrom as if the experience were real; and this feeling is thus highly contributory to that valuation of the experience (incalculably complex, according to our individual background) which completes our "idea" of that experience. We predicted that the method of musical expression, since music is incapable of portraying external fact, would prove to be *a re-*

versal of the direction of this inference — not a direct derivation of feeling from portrayed fact, but (sufficiently for the erection of an idea) an inferential derivation of fact from the portrayal of its feeling-resultant. Our elements appear to be quite literal portrayals of the elemental tensions and motor impulses of feeling. How far the derivation therefrom of an image of external experience is possible, and something of the critical effort which must control that inference will be seen when we put our hypothesis to the test.*

Before we do that, however, another aspect of the whole process of expression — its most obvious aspect, that of performance — must be briefly considered.

Our discussion has dealt with the musical idea to be uttered, and not with the manner of its utterance. That idea, set down in the familiar symbols of musical notation, is far more difficult to apprehend from those signs than is a verbally symbolized idea. Printed words are immediately recognizable as equivalent to those spoken symbols for familiar things and acts through which communications of idea are made. Printed notes, similarly, are really symbols for tones; but even for many experienced musicians they do not evoke images of tone. With instrumental performers, especially on keyboard instruments, they are largely signs for finger-behavior; and it is only when this mechanical act has been performed that the meaning of the tonal symbol is realized. The fact, rather than the purport, of the tonal organization is thus often all that is projected to the hearer.

The word expression thus quite properly refers not merely to the matter but also to the manner of the utterance; and that manner is of the highest import. For the performer must not only utter the thought in its intended syntactical organization; he must set forth its implications, whether of syntax or of more extraneous sense. He is, indeed, the re-creator of the musical composition — the impersonator of the composer himself. To fulfill this role is a high imaginative achievement.

To attain this end, the performer must acquire a great battery of skills — of technical devices contributory to effective and meaningful utterance. Although they are in the highest degree contributory to meaning, none of these devices has in itself any intrinsic meaning-value. They are thus

---

* For a comment on a recent study, *The Language of Music*, by Deryck Cooke (Oxford University Press, 1959), presenting another hypothesis of musical expression than that we shall set forth, see the Appendix (pp. 191–195).

patently secondary factors in the actual process of expression — dependent on and derived from the really elemental suggestions inherent in the musical substance. But we must briefly consider them in that light before our hypothesis — that an image of emotion, sufficiently vivid to be inferentially valued as a reaction to human experience, may be conveyed by the musical substance — is put to the test.

❦ VII ❦

The Secondary Factors of Musical Expression

T H E elements of musical expression — tone-stress and ideal motion, if our identification is accurate — may be so manipulated as to present the musical substance in the aspect of a vehicle through which an idea — an image and a valuation — of extramusical experience may be communicated. This communication is embodied in a structure of tones, also visible purely as structure, just as a verbal communication is embodied in a purely syntactical structure of words. Final determination of the meaning of either communication must obviously be made through precise observation of this structure, both as structure and as vehicle. But even a linguistic communication, if its factual reference is at all complex, and still more if it has emotional implications (e.g., the role of Hamlet), may yield varied images of experience. That is, it must be interpreted.

This is even more true of musical than of verbal communications, because musical symbols (notes), for any but the most accomplished readers, evoke images of tone far less vivid than are the objective images evoked by words.* Musical communications, also, have a much larger emotional component than is usual in verbal utterances, and require a nicety of inflection which words seldom demand. Actual utterance is thus a *sine qua non* of musical interpretation, and the interpreter will appear to bear most of the burden of communication.

To bear this, he must develop highly imposing skills — devices for ut-

* Reading, for competent instrumental performers, is often a kind of facile "pronunciation," accomplished (as with singers of texts in unfamiliar languages) mechanically, and often with but slight understanding of the meaning to be conveyed. The pianist, for example, may identify a printed note primarily as a command to strike a particular key, hearing only after it is struck the tone for which that note was really the symbol. The singer must indeed imagine his interval before he can sing his note; but he is reading only a single melodic line, not the whole texture of the music, and depends on accompanying forces for much of his interpretation.

terance which can be acquired only through arduous training. Faulty utterance, whether of the structural or the extramusical meaning contained therein, will be resented. And although many of the devices the competent interpreter employs were clearly indicated to him by the composer, his reading of the music, if convincing, will so blend his own tonal manipulations with the actual idea of the piece (which was the composer's) that to the hearer the interpreter appears as composer.

He has played or sung "expressively." His devices were essential to expression. Why, then, are they not also *elements* of expression? The fairly evident fact that they are adjuncts, not elements, will appear as soon as the composer is given his rightful place as the true originator of the utterance. It is no disparagement of the importance of the adjuncts to classify them as secondary. This distinction is made for clarity of analysis merely. And the rightness of our distinction will be clearly seen if we examine the devices and their function.

The most conspicuous of the secondary factors are timbre, register, *tempo rubato*, vibrato, shading, and phrasing. The order in which they are here named in no sense indicates the order of their importance, which could hardly be factually determined. They will be observed, however, in that sequence.

Timbre (tone-quality) is perhaps the performer's first concern. Physically, this is a fact of combination, in various degrees of intensity, of partial with fundamental vibrations. But it can be seen thus only in the physical laboratory. It is viewed by performer and listener alike as a simple sensory value. Its grosser features are prescribed, in orchestral and choral writing, by the choice and the number of the instruments or voices employed; but even here, and still more in solo utterance, subtler values are also implied. Since tone-quality is perhaps a more nearly integral factor in the musical utterance than are the values offered by the other devices, we must examine it more minutely.

We found fluctuant tonal tension elemental for expression. Doubtless through their similarity to the fluctuant tensions of the speaking voice, which are highly contributory to verbal meaning, the fluctuant timbres of musical tone may exhibit intrinsic suggestions of tension. Being intrinsic, it may appear that they are really elemental for expression — that they should have been included along with pitch-variation, activity, and dissonance as contributing to the element we are calling tone-stress. They belong, however, in a different category. For those tensions were integral factors of the musical structure itself — the primary vehicle of expression. Their value is thus substantive. But timbre, which must clearly be chosen for its appropriateness to this substantive value, is adjectival — a modifier of the substantive. It is true that, just as adjectives in language often cloak a measure of substantive meaning under the guise of adjectival form (e.g., in the word factual), so the intrinsic tension of timbre may both possess and convey substantive suggestion. Nevertheless, this timbre must be *chosen* — chosen for appropriateness to the substantive image of experience. Its value may indeed be no less significant than that of the substantive which it modifies; but it is essentially an adjectival, and therefore a secondary, contribution. Yet the peculiar vividness of a culminant tonal tension — a moment at which the expressive element of tone-stress is functioning at its highest — would be lost to the hearer if it were not bodied forth in appropriate tonal color. Indeed, an image of experience, primarily defined through the elements, may acquire through appropriate tone-color an immediate sense of reality akin to that which, in language, is effected by onomatopoeia.*

Inappropriateness — less patent as falsity in music than in language, since inappropriate tone may still be highly pleasing as a sensuous stimulus — is of course similarly discriminable only on the ground of that substantive value which we noted a moment ago. But just as we found our Swinburne stanza a weariness to both ear and mind through its superfluous verbal artistry, so it is possible for the performer (and, alas, for the composer as well) to drench his hearers in meaningless tonal exquisiteness (or harshness).

Yet color in music is an intrinsic part of its substance, far more than in language; and its value cannot be measured, unless exceptionally, by the yard-stick of analogy with language. The orchestral palette now embraces as many shades as that of the painter, and it would be folly to ignore the high aesthetic interest of finely discriminated color. Some, indeed, have proposed color as a fourth element of musical structure. It approached that status with the impressionists, and Webern, in his earlier period, seems definitely to have regarded it as such. To those who follow Hanslick in denying to music any power of expression, color may readily appear as elemental; but since to those abstractionists music has no other

---

* Such vividness characterized the performance of our Bach concerto. And I remember, with similar clarity, Edyth Walker's utterance of the words "Treuloser holder!" after the drinking of the love-potion in *Tristan*, as conveying through the tone itself the very essence of Isolde's submission.

value than structure, the question as to what is elemental would seem, for them, largely academic. Color, at any rate in the vast body of accepted musical literature, has been used for its appropriateness; and the ineluctable question, "appropriate to what?" will find its clearest answer to be, not only "to a purpose of design," but also "to a purpose of expression."

Register, definitely prescribed in the texture of the composition, is hardly a resource to be chosen by the performer as appropriate to the thought. Also, when it can be so adapted, it will prove to be suggestive largely through timbre. Yet the analogy between high and low instruments and the four distinct and generally recognized qualities of high and low voices makes possible many unusual intimations of character in tone which strike the ear rather as values of register than of color. The peculiar sonority of a passage played high on the G-string of the violin, for example, is suggestive of a voice speaking in an unusual range, and thus imparting a quality of tension rather than of color. Many varieties of such tension are available to the skilled performer, and are to a considerable extent effects chosen as appropriate to the thought. Low tones, being like low voices, have an immediate suggestion of masculinity. To transfer their characteristic sonority to high register is to impart a peculiarity to the utterance which is only in part a value of color. Unusual combinations of register may also be highly significant. Observe, for example, the opening of Beethoven's *Appassionata* sonata. The theme, unharmonized, is in two voices, two octaves apart. Play the left hand an octave higher than it is written, and you will see the importance of this exceptional choice of register.

Tempo rubato, which is metrically inexact but proportionately symmetrical rhythmic motion (other than that which is involved in longer stretches of *accelerando* or *ritardando*), is obviously a device appropriate to those inflections of musical motion which define, for example, languor or its opposite — nervous over-excitement. But these extremes are by no means the only occasions for which *tempo rubato* is appropriate. One has only to attempt the performance of a well-studied composition in accord with the undeviating tick of a metronome to see that some degree of deviation such as is implied in our definition is essential to natural musical utterance. But metronomic stiffness is resented on no "absolute" ground, but because it fails to correspond with that flexibility of motion in our own bodies (whether the motion be real or imaginal) which again corresponds to our nervous tension, and thus makes ideal motion a credible element of musical expression. Exaggerated, the device is resented on the same ground of unreality.

Vibrato, on string instruments, is a fluctuation of pitch, of indeterminate width, around a given pitch center. In wind instruments it is really a fluctuant dynamic intensity, although its effect is strikingly similar to that produced by the string player. Both may be produced by the singer; but fluctuant pitch is there generally termed a "wobble," and is condemned. Dynamic fluctuation, however, is almost a natural phenomenon, since the maintenance of tension at an unchanging level in the vocal chords, and in the "wind-chest" beneath them, is extremely difficult. Vibrato is nowadays regarded as essential to the effective utterance of melody in most solo instruments as well as in solo voices. It greatly enriches the value of timbre, which itself contributes a kind of naturalness indispensable to expression; but of course it may be exaggerated into grotesqueness.

Shading, although it is often an effect of color, is chiefly accomplished through dynamic gradation. Phrasing, commonly understood as punctuation, is perhaps more exclusively a product of graduated dynamics. The two, however, are so interrelated as to be all but inseparable. For intelligent phrasing is not merely the appropriate punctuation of the melodic line, but is the meaningful "drawing" of that line in every detail. When it is so drawn, a strong impression of color is usually conveyed; yet analysis (and carefully analyzed practice) will show that subtle dynamic gradation is really the chief agent.*

These are the principal devices available to the performer for intensifying the images of tension and motion which we have called elemental for expression. Only through their judicious use can the full expressive sense,

---

* It is commonly and justly observed that the sensitive pianist "colors" his tone. Yet he has no control over that tone except at the one instant when, through his stroke on the key, the hammer strikes the string. And inspection of the mechanism of the action will reveal that single finger-strokes can yield but one variation in tone — that of loudness. The damper-pedal, depressed, adds to the tone thus produced an incalculable increment of sympathetic partial vibrations — actual color-values; the soft pedal causes the hammer to strike two instead of three strings tuned in unison, changing the character of the tone; both are highly contributory to color; but they will not of themselves produce that *effect* of color of which we are speaking.

That effect is nevertheless real. And it has been amply proved that it is in reality produced by an infinite subtlety of dynamic gradation, not merely in the drawing of the melodic line but in the adaptation to that line of the supporting and surrounding harmony. *Tempo rubato*, obviously not in the least a tonal value, often contributes (quite imperceptibly to the hearer) a high completion to the impression of color.

indicated in the printed notation-symbols of a musical composition, be made to come alive for the hearer — made to appear as that metaphor of experience which was uttered by our Bach concerto.

If no more than the tonal substance indicated by that score had been presented to us, there would have been no metaphor — no intimation of experience whatever. If the devices we have just discussed had been applied in a manner appropriate to the syntactical and structural sense of the music only — appropriate, that is to the evocation of an image of purely musical experience — the learned among that audience might have felt that musical experience had itself been limned metaphorically. I cannot prove, of course, that the little group of learned musicians saw anything more in that performance than purely musical experience. But this, as a total group, was a far from learned audience. Our behavior, I can testify, was wholly unanimous. It had none of the ear-marks of that perfunctory approval which, even for highly pleasing efforts, applause usually indicates. There was an undertone in that roar, just as there was an undertone in our long silence, indicative of a common awareness and a common estimate of experience far deeper than that of music itself.

The performer — or rather, the performers, for orchestra and conductor were equally involved — used all the devices we have listed as secondary. Without those devices, the response would have been insignificant. To call them secondary thus seems invidious. Yet, independently of that idea to which they were appropriate, they could not have been displayed at all; and it is only in this aspect of dependence that they must be described as secondary.

They are devices appropriate also to music as music. The elements of expression are also visible as factors of the musical substance. But just as those factors can be so chosen and so designed as to portray knowable features of our neuro-muscular response to stimuli which are not music; just as tone-stress and ideal motion in the guise of tonal organization may work together for the portrayal of states of excitement familiarly aroused by ideas rooted in experience quite unrelated to art; so these secondary factors of musical expression may work together with the elements to enliven the image suggested by those elements into an awareness neither verbal nor musical, but an awareness, nevertheless, of reality.

Our study will be deeply concerned with this awareness of reality. To define reality in this sense is difficult. Quite clearly, reality will be much more than factuality. Objective discrimination between the factual and the non-factual — the real as opposed to the unreal — is a primary step toward the awareness of reality. But even the real — or, to put it less abstractly, an object recognized as real — has *in itself* no attribute which can properly be described as *its* reality. Outside ourselves, where it actually is, it merely exists. Inside ourselves — i.e., in our consciousness — it evokes an awareness of its existence. But that awareness can only be of its existence *as we see it*; and what we call its reality is thus an attribute in some measure supplied by ourselves.

Like objects themselves, the attributes of objects are discriminable as real or unreal. Experience is the fruit of an infinity of observations of this kind. If both observation and discrimination were unfailing — if we possessed a touchstone of reality — the pattern of human existence would long since have been completely laid out, and the problems of existence solved — probably by the self-extinction of a race completely bored by conformity to a pattern. But we have no other touchstone — no other faculty of discrimination — than the mind. Experience soon proves the penalties of false discrimination to be great. Consequently we strive by every available means for just assessment, not only of the factually real as opposed to the false, but of the significant attributes of the real.

In the field of factual reality, science has performed miracles of discrimination. Consequently we pursue its method, even in those wider fields of experience where its explorations are less successful. In this wider field, every man is forced to make — with or without the aid of science — endless discriminations. When factual discrimination ends, he must revert to reason — the faculty which initiated science. But even here he is often compelled to rely on Pascal's "reasons of the heart, of which reason knows nothing."

The heart is sometimes perverse. "I know I'm wrong," it says, "but keep still!" Yet sometimes such intuition turns out to be more right than the principle of insufficient reason that was invoked against it. For intuition may draw from very deep wells of experience. Indeed, our final judgments of reality must draw from those wells, for it is only there that many of its most significant attributes have been registered for consciousness.

Music appears to many to reveal reality. If our hypothesis is sound, the process and something of the substance of that revelation may be seen in the functioning of our elements. To this study, after our overlong preparation, we may now turn.

※ *VIII* ※

The Functioning of the Elements

Our hypothesis, now to be tested, may be summarized briefly as follows:
There are two fundamental elements of musical expression — tone-stress and ideal motion. These elements may serve to portray, respectively, two of the three elemental factors of emotional experience — nervous tension and motor impulse. If the particular types of nervous tension and motor impulse, thus represented, appear as correlative reactions — if both are recognizable as characteristic of the known or naturally imaginable response to a given type of emotional stimulation — then these representations, functioning in combination, may form the ground-work of an intelligible expression of the emotional attitude aroused by exposure to experience. The superstructure of idea erected upon this ground-work remains to be determined.

A variety of secondary factors may enhance the vividness of the elemental suggestions. These secondary factors (timbre, register, dynamic or rhythmic inflection, and the like) have just been rehearsed and their secondary relation to the elements themselves has been demonstrated.

We are now to consider the manner in which, through the functioning of these elements and their accessories, music may offer an intelligble expression of that image and that valuation of experience which, in our view, may properly be said to form an idea. We have demonstrated, so far, no more than a fact of resemblance between music and certain essential features of emotional condition. More than this fact of resemblance must be offered before an actuality of expression is achieved. The representation, like any other, must be interpreted before it can become an idea — a fact of expression. For feeling is not a mere additive compound of nervous tension and motor impulse. It is a highly complex state of consciousness of which nervous tension and motor impulse are characteristic. True expression must somehow reveal or suggest or portray that complex state; and for this end the elements of expression, functioning literally as portrayals of tension and motion, are inadequate.

This admission, however, does not invalidate them as capable agents of expression. No medium of expression has ever been invented which can portray emotional or ideational consciousness in all its complexity. Each art, in consequence, attains expression largely through suggestion, and uses those types of suggestion which are most congenial to it.

The so-called representative arts set forth objective facts chiefly — external things or conditions of objective experience which normally arouse our emotions. These represented things or conditions, whether real or imaginal, consciousness interprets by a kind of inference which determines their immediate or imaginable significance for ourselves.

Music, almost wholly incapable of objective representation, sets forth our normal or imaginable reactions to the objects of experience — in the last analysis, our emotional recognition of their significance. This representation, consciousness also interprets — by a kind of reverted inference which discovers or intuits enough of the causal objective reality to make the portrayed feeling-state appear as a natural product of exposure to experience. But it is perhaps well to repeat, before our demonstration begins, that what music offers in its aspect as a vehicle of expression is a *representation* of knowable facts, characteristic not of objective experience itself but of our consciousness of objective experience; and that music, like all the others, is thus a representative art.*

Since we shall be concerned with rather minute analytical observations of detail in the music chosen for the demonstration of our hypothesis, it may be well to set forth in advance some of the more general conclusions to which our analysis will point. It is evident that the whole area of con-

---

* The abstract painter, rejecting all that is directly representative, is striving through color and design for a truer expression of feeling than could be conveyed if those same general facts of color and design were devoted to the literal representation of some objective "event" whose natural consquence would be the feeling he is trying to express. That feeling may indeed be the delight in form alone, evoked by tensions and cohesions of line and color apparently existent only in those same facts of line and color. (Even these, however, as we suggested in the footnote to page 40, may have more reference to objective reality than he suspects.) But the feeling may also be (as is indicated by the quite objective titles of utterly nonrepresentative paintings) the emotion evoked by quite ordinary and familiar experience — the connotations of Autumn, for instance. The painter is here pursuing precisely the method of expression of the musician, and — in so far as he wishes a consciousness of Autumn to form a part of his observer's response to his picture — he must be interpreted as the musician is interpreted.

sciousness aroused by a work of art will be vastly greater than the area directly stimulated by the detail of that work. This augmentation of the area of response will prove to be the addition, to that immediate and factual awareness, of increments of association. Our final understanding of both the expressive and the formal values of a work of art is thus determined to a great extent by our accumulated store of associable experience — our background. Whether that which the art work represents is objective fact or the feeling correlative to fact, similar increment must be added — out of the observer's own background — if full understanding is to be attained.

There is danger of course, and particularly with music, that the increment thus added will be mere idle association, evoked in an idle mind. The "facts" of feeling are less clearly known than are the facts of objective experience which arouse feeling. We ordinarily identify our emotions, not in terms symbolic of feeling but in immediate images of their objective causes. Consequently, although music represents the subjective fact of feeling more vividly than does any other art, full understanding of that which music literally expresses must in considerable measure depend on that associative increment which is an inference of circumstance. Much more than idle feeling-response — indeed, a keen discrimination of feeling-character — must be comprised in that increment. We shall soon see that a quite sufficient indication of that character may be offered in music which has been composed (as great music is) by a mind aware of this essential discrimination.

The imaginative performer will "visualize" these inferences and will somehow communicate, not his precise visualizations but the essential sense of them, to his hearers. A most illuminating account of this interpretative imagery is offered by Ralph Kirkpatrick in his definitive study of a great composer and his music — *Domenico Scarlatti* (Princeton University Press, 1953, p. 160):

For me, nearly all of Scarlatti's music has some root in the experiences and impressions of real life or in the fantasies of the dream world, but in a fashion that ultimately can be stated only in music. The notions and outwardly ridiculous scenarios which I may suggest to myself or to a pupil in order to heighten a sense of the character of a piece *bear the same relations to performance as did the original real life stimulus to Scarlatti's composition.* After they have served their purpose they must be forgotten in favor of the real music. When perpetuated on paper they become sad and misleading caricatures.

The Scarlatti sonatas . . . have no exact visual or verbal equivalents, but they are an endlessly varied record of experience on constantly shifting levels of gesture, dance, declamation, and remembered sound. They ridicule translation into words, but, with all the vitality that is in them, *they resist any attribution of abstractness.*

The italics are mine. Other commentators might, instead, have italicized "sad and misleading caricatures," and have interpreted the "endlessly varied record of experience" as purely musical. Even the "levels of gesture, dance, declamation, and remembered sound" — the regions of Mr. Kirkpatrick's imagination stimulated by these pieces — might be differently identified by other performers who still repudiated "any attribution of abstractness." But the essential imagery of experience, as here attested by one who is certainly among our foremost interpreters of music, is a product of precisely those tensions and motions of the musical substance which we shall observe as elemental for expression.

With full recognition of the uncertainties inevitable in any attempt to verbalize musical impressions, we shall now try to show, by examining in great detail a few typical examples, that music can convey a generally intelligible expressive sense. We shall first study the contributions made by our still hypothetical elements of expression; then those made by the secondary factors. Being cast in the clumsy vehicle of words, these discussions will be tedious, and the difference in interest between the verbal and the musical aspects of the ideas set forth will be unpleasantly great. We beg the reader, therefore, to keep the primary musical facts as vividly present in the mind as possible, not only that his observation may be clear, but that his critical judgment of our statements may be alert.

As material for illustration we shall present three different types of music: (1) music which is clearly expressive in itself, but which has also a known background of non-musical association against which we can in some measure test the validity of our conclusions; (2) music whose expressive significance, although it is verbally indicated in a general way, is chiefly perceptible in the music itself; and (3) a fugue, for which no authentic verbal explanation or circumstantial background exists.*

* In some measure our choice of illustrative examples will be self-explanatory. Their expressive import, however, may seem too obvious to require analytical demonstration. They are chosen, moreover, from the established literature, and reflect (like our illustrative poetic stanza) conventions of structure and expression nowadays considerably discarded. But the reader will realize that we are not trying to demonstrate the expressive value of these examples, but are trying to show the principles underlying these values. The fact of expression will be demonstrated suf-

The Functioning of the Elements

For the sake of succinctness our first illustration will be a thematic fragment only — not a whole musical composition or even a whole musical sentence. Such themes, however, are the material out of which larger divisions of compositions are constructed, the method being varied repetition. The present fragment is not the first presentation of the theme, but is that (immediately following) in which the whole substance of the thought is first embodied.

We shall observe first the elements and then the secondary factors of expression, so far as these are capable of isolation. We shall try to exhibit them in as factual a light as possible, avoiding suggestions of emotional purport until the detail under scrutiny has revealed the elemental forces of tension or motion resident in it. Thereafter, however, we shall draw such inferences as the substance seems to warrant.

Our first example is from Wagner:

Ex. 1

Because the motor outlet of emotion is more clearly perceptible than is nervous tension, and since the element of ideal motion is therefore more clearly visible than that of tone-stress, we shall reverse the order in which our elements were discovered and shall discuss first the element of ideal motion.

The image of motion is here evoked, not by marked rhythmic pulses but by the continuous flow of the melodic line. Every detail of that line is thus significant. The long initial A♭, unimpeded, but also unimpelled by any external rhythmic factor, undergoes a sort of tremor (the "turn" in 32nd notes) which itself may seem to be the impulse that causes the melody to rise to the high F — the moment of greatest rhetorical (but not rhythmic) stress in the theme. Motion more fluid and effortless than this is unimaginable. The melodic point that we may suppose to be tracing the line

ficiently if the process of expression is established. It will be seen that if our hypothesis is sound, it may guide critical study in a very wide field of musical utterance.

poises itself here, at the peak of the curve, for a time (a dotted quarter) as long as was its easy flow before the tremor began; and this maintenance of an achieved height is characteristic of the whole curve of motion. (Imagine the F as an 8th note. The whole purport of the effortless A♭ and its fluid rise will be changed.) For the dip to C is followed by another rise (to E♭); and the final swift descent (it seems swift because of the long drop to F) completes an undulant curve in which the ease and fluidity we noted are only once abated (with the E♭, whose value we shall have to examine more minutely).

This will suffice to fix in our minds an image, not merely of the melodic path but of the propulsive force resident in the melody itself. Yet we must ask, if there is no external rhythmic propulsion, whence comes the effortless energy with which the melody moves? Are there tonal influences within the melody itself which may account for this power — influences which are perhaps contributory to motion, even though their primary value may be that of tone-stress? Energy and direction in the moving point which we imagine as tracing a melodic line are facts readily classifiable as in the category of ideal motion. Yet even the relation of height to depth in pitch was first noted as a fact of tone-stress; and similar contributions to the whole suggestion of motion may appear in tone-relations which are primarily values of tension.*

Such a value, indeed, appears at once. We described active and rest tones as primarily suggestive of tension; but they also palpably imply motion. We may then find here what we have so far sought in vain — an explanation for the rising energy of the rhythmically unpropelled A♭. This music is in the key of E♭, where the rest tones are E♭, G, and B♭. Every note in the theme, therefore — save for the two 32nds, G and B♭ (which are so swift that their rest value is hardly perceptible) and the E♭ (which is *made* active by the harmony) is an active tone. At its very outset the A♭ is established (largely by its harmony) as active. (Strictly, it should

---

* The difficulty we encountered in attempting to define the elements of expression as discrete facts of tone-stress and motion here rises (and not for the last time) to plague us. For these are not wholly discrete facts. They are allied as attributes — indeed, they are alloyed as constituents — of the activated musical substance we are studying. Similarly, nervous tension and its allied muscular contractions are alloyed constituents of the activated human organism. If this human activation were merely the automatic response to a stimulus, it would have little interest and its musical correlative would have less. But human activations may be purposeful; their purpose, communicated as idea, may be widely significant; and the vehicle of communication — however confusing the analysis of its alloyed substance or the process of its communication — may be of corresponding value.

progress to the nearest rest tone. Actually, indeed, it does so; but the G —
and also the B♭ — quickly passed over, not only show no rest but rather
reveal in their tremor of haste the intensity of propulsion already inherent
in the A♭.) This drive is patently strong enough to effect with ease the
upward leap to F; but it is hardly accounted for by the mere fact of activity
in the note.

By the principle governing the progression of active tones, the descent
from F should be to the rest tone, E♭; and again it is so, but circuitously,
in a gracious dip and rise whose shallower curve is not only exquisite as
line in continuation of the soaring leap preceding, but is a vivid sign of
the quantum of energy that remains, after the F, in the moving melodic
point. The descent from E♭ to F, however, has a feeling of compulsion,
due not merely to the implications of direction in the preceding curve, but
also to the artificial activity of the E♭ itself.

So far, we have tried to confine our observation to the facts of motion
portrayed by the theme. Inevitably, however, that sort of propulsion
inherent in the fact of activity in tonal relations had to be considered.
There is still more of propulsion to be noted; but this may now be subsumed under the first of our elements of expression — the fact of tone-
stress as a portrayal of nervous tension.

We spoke of the initial A♭ as unpropelled. Viewed merely melodically
it is so. But there is in the harmony a certain degree of dissonance — a
tonal tension significant for attendant nervous excitement, but also appropriate for the initiation and the maintenance of the motion we have
observed in our ideal melodic point. So fluid a motion, in a curve so gracious, could never be the product of violent nervous excitement. And the
harmony here supporting the melody is not only gently propulsive of that
melody; it contributes similarly to the portrayal of that state of nervous
tension which the composer intended, but which we are forbidden to consider until our account of the elemental contributions as facts is complete.

There is but one unchanging harmony supporting the whole theme.
This is the chord of the dominant (major) ninth. Comprising no half-step
discord, this harmony is soft, not harsh; having five notes of different
letter-name, it is rich; having as its root a primary tone (the dominant), it
imparts a certain quietude. (It is this chord which makes unmistakable the
tonic, and hence establishes the activity and rest we have described in
the melodic notes.) These qualities of softness, richness, and quietude
persist unaltered until the fourth beat of the measure. (The general slight

crescendo prescribed by the composer heightens but does not change the character of the tension.) But at the fourth beat the highest of the underlying harmonic notes (D) moves upward to E♭, providing not only a new dissonance but also the first audible rhythmic impulse to be heard since the beginning. The dissonance is still not harsh, for there is no half-step harmonically sounded; but E♭ is foreign to the sustaining ninth-chord, is made active by that harmony, and its activity is at once transferred to the ensuing melodic E♭. But when this note appears in the melody, taken by skip from C, on the strong beat of the measure and (in spite of its dissonance) appearing as the natural note of resolution of the dissonant high F, we feel a tiny stab of harmonic pain that, slight as it is, is enough to account for the sudden drop of the melodic line to the low F.

The reader is doubtless appalled at the use of so many words to describe nine notes of melody and a single underlying harmony. We can only ask him — so far as is necessary by playing, but ultimately by *thinking* all the detail of this music (for it is not easy to utter) — to translate our clumsy descriptions into musical concepts. The expressive qualities we are observing are in the music, not in our words, and neither ideal motion nor tone-stress nor the accessory values still to be studied can be rightly sensed until the substance of the music is felt as a living musical thought. Our microscopic examination has magnified all these details by several hundred diameters. No ordinary act of hearing could assimilate all this complexity of suggestion at its magnified value and at the normal rate. Yet, like the etymologies of words, unnoted in ordinary speech, those contributory values are *there*, and even when seen in their natural proportions they affect our perception of the whole value to which they contribute. (Our considerably minute examination of the poetic stanza by no means accounted for every value to be found there.)

We have now sufficiently considered the elemental suggestions of nervous tension and motor impulse as they appear in their musical guise. We have offered as little expressively interpretative comment as possible, since we must later observe the interpretative process as a separate fact. But it may be well, before going on, to sort out and arrange the many varied impressions we have received, classifying them into the two general groups indicated by the nature of the elements themselves. These impressions, if our hypothesis is sound, are the raw material of emotional representation. The secondary factors, still to be observed, should clarify these impressions and intensify them. How these elemental and accessory suggestions unite to convey a considerably vivid image of experience and its attendant valuation will then be shown.

We have found in the music, thus far:

1. A representation of motion, effortless and poised, which through a single impediment loses, at the end, something of the eager freedom with which it began.

2. Representations of stress of three sorts:

a. Tonal relations of height and depth, intrinsically suggestive of alternate tension and relaxation, but here concrescent toward a single impression of feeling character. At the same time these relations of height and depth suggest a path of melodic motion appropriate to that character.

b. Tonal relations of melodic activity and rest, more vividly suggestive of intrinsic tensions of feeling, and defining throughout the impulses which determine the melodic path.

c. Tonal relations of harmonic dissonance, almost unaltered, yielding the sensuous impressions of richness, sweetness, and softness, but at the same time providing a certain quantum of motor energy.

Assuming that the music is intended to suggest or portray emotion, it will be agreed that such ease and grace of motion, and such exquisitely graduated and combined tonal tensions may depict an emotion pleasurable rather than painful. Leaving the reader to circumscribe for himself the particular region of pleasure thus indicated, we may observe the contribution of the secondary factors to the definition of that region.

The tremulous vibrato of the tympani, growing into the tremolo of the violas at the second bar, is hardly a fact of propulsion, but it does portray a characteristic of motion — a kind of persistent underlying tremor. The clarinet, which has the important inner progression D–E♭–F, here passes from the thicker *chalumeau* to its lighter middle register; the horns, bassoon, and bass clarinet which sustain the harmony are smooth and mellow in tone; and the theme itself, against this background, is sounded in the clear vibrant beauty of the violins. These values of tone were prescribed in general by the composer, but they are intensified through the discrimination of finely trained performers for their appropriateness, certainly to the musical phrase itself and possibly to the more than musical thought which the phrase utters.

The nature of that thought and the process of its evocation are at last brought into the foreground as the real object of our inquiry. We have described, as factually as we were able, intimations of tension, motion, and timbre inherent in the stuff of the music. They are characteristic of a phrase of music intelligible as a purely musical phrase. With our attention directed solely to this musicality, they may be accepted as no more than this. Yet these details, observed individually, have each a certain interest for an organism capable of emotion. They appear, indeed, as correlatives or even representations of knowable emotional reactions. They also appear as in some measure cognate. As we have described them, however, they do not add up to a sum recognizable as either an image or a valuation of experience.

They do, nevertheless, portray fragments of such an idea — familiar characteristics of the feeling with which we react to external experience. Such reactions form no small part of that valuation of experience which, we are contending, is one essential factor of an idea.

Such valuations normally arise as instantaneous inferences or deductions drawn either from actual or portrayed experience — deductions indicative of the significance *for us* of the experience itself, and thus wholly appropriate to our awareness of the experience. We made such a deduction from the portrayed encounter between Richard Feverel and Lucy. But if it had been possible to portray in words the reaction to that encounter instead of the encounter itself, we might well have found it possible to deduce therefrom not, of course, the physical detail of the encounter, but certainly all that was essential for an imaginative reconstruction of the scene.* Let us then attempt to transfer into terms of actual or imaginative experience the hints of motion, tone-stress, and color which we have so laboriously accumulated.

The motion of our theme, untrammeled, poised, and effortless, may be visualized as a curve traced by some ideal object (we called it a melodic point) in ideal space. That curve, with little additional effort of the imagination, may appear as the path along which we ourselves have flown. What awareness of experience — what state of being — could arouse in us such an image of motion? For the music does more than delineate this exquisite pattern. It commands us to enact imaginatively this physically impossible flight. Considered thus — not statically as mere line, but dynamically as spiritual impulse — it can hardly suggest less than a condition of ecstasy: of being indeed outside oneself.†

* Such a reconstruction — confessedly manufactured, and merely illustrative — is the imaginative deduction of implied experience made by Mr. Kirkpatrick from music far less directly purposive toward emotional expression than that which we are studying, and described on p. 89.

† We used this same word to characterize a state induced by our Bach concerto.

But there is also portrayed in the music a condition of nervous tension, in part propulsive (as we have seen) of the motion we enacted. On the level of sensation merely, we found warmth and richness — values readily correlated with our image of flight. What state of mind or feeling is as warm and rich as this; is expectant, as the gentle persistence of dissonance in this theme is expectant; and is tinged with pain as this music is tinged by the darker throb of the two E♭'s? For so strong are the initial impressions of warmth and ecstasy, and so gently is the sense of pain blended with them, that there is here no hint of bitterness or foreboding but only the agony of overmuch delight.

The not too critical reader will doubtless resent, at this point, a digression from the path of inference we are now pursuing. But we are asking for critical assent to our proposition, and must pause to consider plausible objections to our argument.

To a considerable extent, what we have just set forth is an individual interpretation of the suggestions of motion and tension offered by this music. The purist (even though this music is by Wagner, whose purpose was unmistakably expressive) may prefer to view these indubitable facts of motion and tension as attributes of the musical substance merely — as facts of textural interest, but in no way valid as stimulations to inference. Or he may accept such hints of character as aberrant excursions, away from the true purpose of music, which leave only a tainted residue of musical purity.

Nor, if such inference as we are drawing be recognized as legitimate, can it be denied that it must be drawn from the individual listener's store both of experience and of imaginative sensibility, and will to that extent be unpredictable. Even the musical sensibility of composers is seldom equally keen for all the resources of musical stimulation. Some are predominantly rhythm-minded (as was Beethoven); some are harmony-minded (as was Wagner); some are melody-minded (as was Verdi). And the public, having the same varieties of disposition but little opportunity of mitigating them by study, must suffer corresponding limitation of its intuitive powers. Thus a rhythm-minded hearer, stimulated chiefly by the motor aspect of our example, might interpret the music as suggesting a joyous but by no means boisterous dance. He who is harmony-minded,

The *whole* awareness is here different — because the implied experience is different. But for that part of the awareness with which we are now dealing, the word is still etymologically appropriate.

on the other hand, drowned in the richness and color of the ninth-chord, might be held moveless in some self-awakened vision of fragrant night. Such fantasy, although not groundless, may remain uncurbed. In that case other expressive suggestions may be largely or wholly obliterated. It is thus clear that unless each expressive factor is observed at its just value, no more may be hoped for in the reactions of a group of untrained individuals than a variety of irreconcilable notions as to the "meaning" of any musical composition.*

Our present example was created by a mature artist of high imaginative invention. It was definitely intended as the musical embodiment of feeling intelligible to any keen observer of the dramatic situation in which it appears. Its every factor probably satisfied the composer's demand, whether critical or more swiftly intuitive, for appropriateness to that situation. (There is probably nothing irrelevant, that is, in the utterance.) We have attempted to weigh, for itself, each contributory factor. We have, as the verbal counterpart of each factor, one or more affective words, such as ecstasy, anticipation, warmth, poignance, together with various qualifications of these things offered by the accessory factors of expression. If we attempt to fuse all these together into a single impression of feeling-character, it will not be difficult to identify the experience with which this music must be associated. This is patently a type of love-music.

But is this all? Have we here love-music in general, suited to every manifestation of that passion? Or will our analysis have revealed in the

* A variety of psychological experiments have been recorded, designed to reveal the degree of unanimity in mass reactions to music. Six or eight short compositions are played, the listener being asked to enter in the appropriate place on his score-sheet that one of a considerable number of listed words which seems to him most appropriate to the piece. The variety or unanimity in the selection of these words is apparently accepted as an index of the unanimity of impression felt by the group.

Such experiment seems to me valueless. In the first place, each of the compositions, since it is played complete, naturally exhibits a considerable variety of emotional character; and the listener may well choose his word to accord with the most verbally vivid out of a large number of suggestions received. In the second place, the word-list may contain nothing that seems to the listener appropriate to his impression; yet he is forced to enter one of these words in his provided space. Moreover, there is no certainty that these bare words, suggestive of feeling but completely without context, have the same meaning value for all readers.

After voicing this objection and suggesting that the subject should be allowed to use his own words, and after insisting that the music should stop after one definite impression of character had been conveyed by the music, I once played six characteristic fragments on the piano for a group of five rather eminent psychologists who happened to be in my office. They were amazed at the unanimity of their response.

substance of the music a definition also of the possible circumstances under which such love as this can occur? Love is tender; but have we here the languishing tenderness of Tristan and Isolde in the garden? Love is eager and expectant; but have we in the hesitant, wondering expectancy of this music any hint of the insatiable eagerness of Isolde as she quenches the torch? Love is ecstatic; but is this the piteous, self-forgetting ecstasy of Isolde as she sings her life out in the *Liebestod?*

We know at once, *from the music itself*, that the passion here portrayed burns in the heart of quite another character than Isolde. Yet we find, in that same portrayal, something strange to our own experience. This love is too simple in essence, too lacking in physicality, and above all *too young* to be quite credible as the experience of one living on the ordinary plane of passion. Still, to think of this love as young, in the sense of immature and callow, is also impossible. This is no childish dream. It bears an unmistakable stamp of mature reality. The creature who loves thus, we must infer, is someone not quite human.

We can test this inference. We are supposed to have heard the earlier dramas of the *Ring* cycle. The history of Brünnhilde's defiance of Wotan is fresh in our minds. We have seen her bound in that enchanted sleep from which she may be awakened only by him who dares to pass through her surrounding ring of fire. We have seen that awakening. Brünnhilde is now no longer the war-maiden. She is a woman — the woman from whom Wotan's kiss took godhood away, and in whom Siegfried's kiss has awakened both humanity and love. Could language or any other medium of utterance than music contrive so instantaneous an embodiment of the passion of a woman for whom both love and the world have been new-created?

That it was Wagner's purpose to portray something of this sort cannot be doubted. The dawn, after the dark foreboding of the Norn-scene, is the dawn not only of day but of Brünnhilde's womanhood. Our understanding of that scene, however, comes from knowledge of events that are neither portrayed nor directly implied in this music. What was implied was feeling — a valuation of those events, realizable only in their light.

But further implications will at once be suggested by this example. This intimation was conveyed by a design — a formed pattern of musical tones.* The tensions and the motor impulses we have described exist in

* Such designs, memorized as static musical patterns and given titles which associate them no longer with the emotion they portray but with the person who felt

this design. Is it possible that a given feature of this design, repeated recognizably in another pattern and in another context, may still retain something of its original expressive value? May this feature of design be used — may it have been used — for a cognate expressive purpose by many composers? It is indeed incumbent upon us to show that something of a given expressive value (e.g., a motor impulse) does persist in essential similarities of design; for unless it were so our elemental factor of ideal motion could hardly be accepted as elemental.

This can be briefly done. Let us consider again, as the elemental suggestion most readily visible, the factor of ideal motion. In the Brünnhilde motive, we found that motor impulse which was conveyed by the opening long note, the turn, and the upward leap thereafter, to be immediately suggestive of the whole impression completed by the ensuing notes. Precisely the same melodic pattern, moving at almost identical speed but with every supporting factor altered, including the very different conclusion, occurs in the familiar theme from *Rienzi* (Ex. 2). Remembering always

Ex. 2

that we are considering here only the motor aspect of the music, observe that the first note is here the tonic of the key instead of the active subdominant (A♭) in the Brünnhilde theme. Neither is there any harmonic propulsion whatever, either in the note itself or in the two beats of tonic harmony which underlie it. Rhythmic propulsion, however, is strongly provided on these two beats, and their march-like drive is continued throughout the fragment. Hence the energy for the leap to B is external, not intrinsic. That note is indeed harmonized (as was the high F) by a dominant ninth-chord; but that harmony, now emerging out of the inert

the emotion (or the thing which generated it), become the *Leitmotive* of the Wagnerian interpreters who write guides to the operas. (Wagner himself never used this term, nor understood his musical motives in this bald and literal sense. His word was *Grundthema* — basic theme.) This one is generally called the "second Brünnhilde motive" — with what loss of meaning, either here or on its later appearances, our discussion will perhaps suggest.

tonic, gives to the B a sense of strain quite lacking in the effortlessly attained F. (The ninth-chord, now in its first inversion, is also more unstable than the other, based on its root.) The rest of the melodic curve shows no such undulation as that in the Brünnhilde motive. Indeed, such motion would have been quite incongruous with this beginning; for the one moment of high tension is all that the stability of the initial tonic chord could well admit, since that stable harmony really governs all the rest of this theme, as the unstable harmony governed the other.

We are really concerned, however, to discover how much of the character we found in the figure from the Brünnhilde theme is discoverable therein in its new context. We found the word ecstasy appropriate to — although by no means fully descriptive of — the first figure. Here, at least in its former sense, it will not do at all. This is no love-music. The mood is sober and depressed; but within that mood, and suggested almost wholly by this figure, there is an upward thrust of urgency which, along with the ensuing depression, imparts to the whole utterance a quality of immediacy akin to desperation.* But he who despairs may be as far outside himself as he who loves.

We have seen the upward thrust of our figure, regarded chiefly in its motor aspect, contributing to a portrayal of depression. In the following (Ex. 3), from Bach's *Well-tempered Clavichord*, Book I, its native buoyancy, with hardly an attendant hint of other feeling, is established at once and, in the second bar (whose first half is a variant of our figure) it continues with the leaping sixths to dominate the whole theme. The initial

Ex. 3

note, G♯ (still a rest tone but now dominant, not tonic, and so less stable), is short and unaccented. The figure of the turn, in consequence, is not a tremor of anticipation emerging from within the initial note. It is a de-

* The theme, as here presented, is from the overture to the opera. In the drama, it appears at the opening of the last act, as the most characteristic phrase of a prayer. All Rienzi's hopes face catastrophe, and his only resource is heaven. This music, of course, will not endure comparison with the Brünnhilde theme, but that comparison is not in question. We are concerned with the intrinsic value of suggestion inherent in a single phrase. Wagner's text for the close of the prayer runs: *Mein Herr und Vater, o blicke herab! . . . erhöre mein tief-inbrünstig Fleh'n.* Desperation, certainly, is in the words. We are contending merely that an element of the emotional state of desperation is also in the music.

lightful antic in itself. It is propelled, indeed, by the very shortness of that initial note (elongate the G♯ merely to a quarter-note and the melody will lose all its lilt) so that the culminant E♯, instead of suggesting a moment of attainment to be dwelt on, merely steps downward to C♯ to complete the dainty motion-pattern. Has insouciance ever been more delightfully portrayed? And has it not also its element of ecstasy?

A franker utterance of the same primary feeling-tone will be found in Ex. 4 from Weber's *Freischütz*. The frankness lies not only in the long initial note (again, the dominant) but in the similar dwelling on the rest-

Ex. 4

tones C and E as points of attainment toward which the turn is now twice employed. An assumption that the interval of the sixth, from G to E, although attained through an intervening point of rest, is similar to the leap of a sixth taken at once as in our other examples, may appear factitious. But that same leap, uninterrupted (as at B in the illustration), forms the climax of the whole utterance. Since the music is from a drama, the purpose of the phrase is unmistakable. Agathe, awaiting her long-delayed lover, has at last heard his footsteps. But one who has heard only the familiar overture to the drama will recognize the immediate joyousness of the phrase as appropriate to her sudden certainty. We have adopted the verbal symbol, ecstasy, as the best available definition of the feeling we are discussing; but again it is apparent that the music defines our word far better than our word defines the music.

Finally, as we have already noted, the same figure appears in the culminant portion of the duet in the second act of *Tristan* (see Ex. 5). Its

Ex. 5

suitability at that moment is obvious. Yet the feeling there expressed is very different from that which we found in the heart of Brünnhilde, so that many differences appear, both in the background of the theme and in the pattern itself. For the pattern is not, in the Tristan music, a separately announced, carefully prepared theme. Rather, it appears as if spontaneously, representing the last incandescence of a passion whose gradual exaltation toward the idea of "night" as the only region habitable by these two stricken souls has been fully set before us. In all the notes of the figure save the turn, accordingly, the music has a swiftness that would ill accord with the quiet ecstasy of Brünnhilde. Neither is there time or space for that quiet undulation which in her theme follows the turn. The tension is now too high for more than the immediate descent from the peak of the curve of motion. The harmony, also, is highly active, is constantly shifting its tonality, and is thus far more varied in color. The figure itself, moreover, is somewhat obscured in prominence because it seldom occurs in the voices, but is mostly kept in the orchestra where it is overridden by the long, passionate phrases of the singers. And when this figure reappears in the *Liebestod* it is not to be understood as transformed into agony. It has indeed for us, the listeners, the pathos which the great poet spoke of as the bitterest of griefs, for it brings into the scene of death the memory of joy. But for Isolde, now actually attaining that *höchste Lust* which she and Tristan had glimpsed in their duet, it is truly ecstasy.

Endless further examples might be cited to show that kindred emotional states have often been portrayed, by different composers, in kindred musical terms. Our single illustrative phrase seems to possess an intrinsic value of suggestion, capable of contributing variously, according to its context, to total impressions of feeling-character vastly more comprehensive than that suggestion, observed for itself alone, could have conveyed. We are trying to show that such suggestion — however diverse the experiences involved in the total impression — is conveyed by agencies we have called elemental for expression. Verbal equivalents (such as our word ecstasy) for total impressions or their details prove extremely unstable. (If language has but a feeble vocabulary for feeling-states, it is still more indigent when details or contributory factors of those states are in question.) Yet an analogy with language, and especially with the etymological values of word-roots is strongly suggested in the various meanings we have found in our illustrative phrase. Indeed, the variations in expressive character we have just been observing are hardly less great than are the variations of meaning in the root (*logos* — a word) found in such familiar combinations as *log*ic, pro*logue*, ana*logy*, or *log*arithm.

Having presented examples in which our hypothetical element of ideal motion was chiefly considered, we should logically go on to show that similar tone-stresses, like similar depictions of ideal motion, have similar expressive values. On any large scale, this is impossible; for the *same* combinations and successions of tonal stress, pursued even for a short time, or repeated at any length, would be repellent.*

In fact, the tone-stresses of music are so widely and subtly variable that our classification of them in the three categories of height-depth, activity-rest, and dissonance-consonance relations is all that can be offered in the way of stress-valuation. It is comparatively seldom that any single chord, or any other type of tone-stress will be found to have constant value in different situations. The simpler dissonances — e.g., the dominant seventh chord — may occur in so many relations, their preparation and resolution may be so diverse, and their position in the musical sentence so variable, that no positive degree of intensity can be ascribed to them. Extremer discords probably do have a more precise suggestiveness. The dominant ninth is more positively characteristic than the dominant seventh, and "secondary" ninths (those built on other notes than the dominant) are more definite in character than the dominant ninth. Schubert uses the chord of the augmented sixth almost as if it were a leading-motive for spiritual pain. But the very subtlety and range of musical expression would be hopelessly narrowed if specific chords or any other facts of tone-stress were to acquire fixed values of expressive suggestion. They would become (as the augmented sixth with Schubert was in danger of becoming) specific symbols — musical words; the ear would weary of their sensation and the mind of their implied meaning; and the loss to the musical language would be nowise compensated for by such artificial definiteness. The really significant value of stress (or of its absence, which may be equally contributory to expression) must be left free if that degree and that relativity of tension is to be built up which is appropriate to the subtle image of experience it is the composer's purpose to convey.

To contrive such appropriateness as this while at the same time pur-

* The formulas of cadence offer at least an example of such monotony. Essential as they are for musical syntax, cadence progressions have troubled composers of all historic periods. Authentic and plagal cadences (essentially, dominant–tonic or sub-dominant–tonic progressions), have provided perfunctory closes for musical sentences ever since the present scheme of tonality was established. Until harmony began to expand its tonal range, these were not much avoided or disguised. Bach, for the extreme of finality, sometimes boldly drops a whole major seventh (e.g., B *down* to C) instead of rising a minor second (B *up* to C) to reach a close on the tonic. At the turn of the twentieth century, dissonant closes (e.g., B major mingled with C major, in Strauss's *Also sprach Zarathustra*, or a major seventh chord, such as closes Ravel's *Jeux d'eaux*) became common. But these devices are rather appropriate to the general idiom then in use than expressive in any real sense.

suing the normal syntactical outline of intelligible musical discourse is a vastly more difficult imaginative feat than is the mere observance of principles of syntactical structure. If we could see what a great composer has *not* written — if we could know by what process of rejection (which is a part of the process of choice) he has arrived at the final form of an expressive utterance — we should have a more valuable lesson in the creative act of musical composition than can be found in any text-book. For our text-books deal with the mechanics of structure as if construction were the creative act.* We cannot, of course (unless, very exceptionally, by a study of such stages in composition as are revealed in Beethoven's sketchbooks) know what a composer has rejected, or why he has rejected it.† For the purpose, not only of the rejections but of the whole creative act, may lie primarily outside the field of structure and somewhere within the field of common, non-musical experience; the discovery of that purpose is then a part of the discovery of musical value; and a just estimate of musical value will be an estimate of the relation of structure to expressive purpose.

The examples so far studied have been with one exception (the Bach theme) indubitably related to non-musical experience. (The Bach theme appears, in the light of our analysis, to be similarly related.) That relation has thus been fairly easy to perceive. Yet the substance we studied has been, in every instance, a *musical* structure; and its communication of non-musical meaning, although made relatively easy because the non-musical experience involved was known in non-musical (verbal) terms, was conveyed through that structure. It is now time to test the validity of that sort of communication in cases where the verbal definition of the experience is less precise.

---

* Stravinsky, as we have seen (cf. p. 10) insists that construction *is* the creative act. Yet he himself acknowledges in that act a quite non-musical purpose — that of revealing "the co-ordination between man and time." Although I must confess a considerable difficulty in understanding that phrase merely as a proposition, and still more in understanding how music can reveal its meaning, I believe I may rightly insist that the phrase symbolizes an idea — an image and a valuation of experience (certainly non-musical) — and that his purpose is therefore not primarily constructive but expressive.

† Beethoven's first sketches for themes which later show tremendous import often appear quite banal. But do these represent all that was in his mind at that first creative moment? It seems more likely that they were literally *memoranda* (things which must be remembered) — hints of a vision already vivid, but not yet "translated" into music.

MUSIC OF VERBALLY SUGGESTED CONTENT

The objection may plausibly be urged against all our illustrative effort thus far that, since the original expressive purpose was known, the conclusions of our investigation were themselves predetermined and were therefore valueless. We did show, however, that in each of the variants of the motion-pattern originally examined a different feeling character was portrayed, while at the same time that one motion-pattern retained, like a word-root affected by various prefixes or suffixes, a certain residual and apparently ineradicable value of suggestion.

We shall now observe what may be called the reverse of this process of analysis. Instead of taking a single musical pattern and exploring its "root meaning" as a factor in a variety of experiences, we shall take two examples of music which deal, unmistakably, with the same experience, and shall try to trace the functioning of our elements toward the portrayal of what will prove to be two widely different "valuations" of that experience. The experience contemplated is death; it is represented under the aspect of that stately ritual — the march — through which men have long found expression for their attitude toward that event; and the surfaces of the two observances of the appropriate ritual are highly similar. The two pieces are from Beethoven's *Eroica* symphony and Chopin's Sonata in B flat minor.

Assuming that our process of analysis has been intelligibly set forth, we shall enter somewhat less minutely into detail and shall thus proceed somewhat more rapidly than in the preceding study. We shall also be less careful to reject our own personal judgments of musical meaning. The reader will accordingly supply our omissions and criticize our inferences as seems best to him. A few bars from the great March in the *Eroica* will suffice. (See Ex. 6, on the opposite page.)

As before, we shall consider first the element of ideal motion.

As the absence of rhythmic propulsion was important, in the Brünnhilde motive, for the suggestion of freedom of movement, so its presence is here significant as conveying the opposite sense. The manner in which that rhythmic energy is applied is notable. The first six bars of this theme begin with notes of identical and impressive length — notes which absorb into themselves the considerable propulsive force supplied by the appoggiatura figure in the basses and by the initial up-beat, so that the weight of these notes is extraordinary. But that force is all but exhausted in the one rhythmic thrust, so that the third and fourth beats (counting the time

Ex. 6

as 4-8, not 2-4) must themselves gather momentum to reach the next strong beat. Dotted 16ths here precede 32nds, giving, in the slow tempo, a sense of laboriousness to the ascent; and this sense is augmented by the fall of the long E♭ to C.

There is also significant contribution to the laborious motion in the simple relation of height and depth in pitch. The effortful ascent we just noted covers no more than a minor third, from C to E♭ (the B♮ is too short to create the tension of the diminished fourth); the same rhythmic thrust that propelled the low G is again imparted to the E♭; but so heavy is this note that it absorbs that energy and can do no more than fall back to C. The ensuing moment of silence after the "feminine" phrase-end, seen merely as an aspect of the ideal motion we are considering, is a vivid contribution to that portrayal. For the characteristic rhythmic thrust on the following high G gives to that note, in comparison to all the preceding tones, an almost explosive energy. But again this energy is absorbed into the note, and the descent, now almost precipitous, is made by 32nds *preceding* dotted 16ths — a vivid inversion of the motion-pattern of ascent in bar 2.

Our somewhat obscure term — ideal motion — for the elemental impression of motion character conveyable by music seems to us here to come quite clear. The whole sense of forward progression in the musical substance (to which the tone-stresses will contribute greatly) is extremely retarded. Its motion is dragged and weighted, heavy-footed and slow; yet the sense of underlying energy is abundant, so that there is no rhythmic sense of weakness or defeat.

Turning now to the values suggested by the tone-stresses, we find the points of activity and rest clearly in accord with, and strongly contributory to, the impressions of motion. We have already had to observe the primary tensions of height and depth to account for some of the values of motion. Observing the melodic notes as active or rest tones, we see that the accented notes in the first phrase (two bars) are *all* rest tones. This stability contributes greatly to that sense of weight which we found to be illustrated by the music in its motor aspect. In the second phrase this sense is heightened. The implication of the high G — a rest tone, attacked out of silence — is wonderfully subtle. (Imagine any active note in its place — for example, an A♭ — and consider the immediate loss in dignity and character!) It pulls downward with all the force of an active tone; and that downwardness is intensified by the placing of the rhythmic accent on the active 32nds which gain only a precarious foothold on the unaccented (dotted 16th) rest tones to which they fall.

The melodic progression E♭–D in the fourth bar forms a kind of rhythmic rhyme to the E♭–C in bar 2. The active note D forms a half-cadence with a feminine ending and, as the first really conspicuous active note thus far, warns the ear of the generally active phrase that is to follow. Indeed, until the final measure, the accented notes are now almost all active tones. The high A♭ is the parallel of the earlier explosive G; but this note is not approached by leap, nor is it attacked out of silence. Its intensity is prepared for by step-wise progression on dotted 16ths (active) followed by 32nds (rest tones), and although it conveys an indubitable sense of pain, its momentary outcry is dominated at once by the extraordinary firmness of the conclusion of the whole theme. This solidity is portrayed by the rythmically even (not dotted) 16ths of the seventh bar — a fact of ideal motion which we did not observe when dealing with that element of expression, since it was hardly necessary to comment further on that aspect of bars 5–8.

The third aspect of tone-stress — that of harmonic consonance and dissonance — is similarly striking. For the first four bars, except at the half-cadence, there is no other harmony than the minor tonic chord. Although it is unrelieved, it imparts great firmness and dignity. Instead of appearing monotonous, it supports and enhances the directness of the melodic utterance, precluding any suggestion of over-weighted misery or nervous abandon. But even here the maintenance of the single harmony produces no impression of stolidity. A singular accumulation of tension is achieved by presenting the one chord in its successive inversions. (The bass, for two bars, is C, the root of the chord; then — approached by two 32nds in a pattern like that of the preceding appoggiatura-figures — it is E♭; then it is G, giving the unstable, almost dissonant 6-4 chord at the half-cadence.) This simplicity in the use of the single harmony for the whole first clause makes effective the use, for the ensuing active melody, of an equally simple active harmony — that of the diminished seventh;* but that melodic sturdiness which appears with the even 16ths is again accompanied by primary triads, so that the cadence, harmonically as well as rhythmically, is on a note of resolute firmness.

This is more than mere marching-music for the dead. Its solemnity is as profound as its sadness. Grief permeates every note and every rhythmic step; but there is no yielding — no indulgence in the alleviating misery of tears. It comprehends heroically and is unafraid.

The title *Marcia funèbre* is wholly appropriate to this music — and wholly needless. That is true also of the Chopin march, to which we now turn (Ex. 7). This music is so familiar that to analyze it at all may seem to the reader a gratuitous adventure in boredom. We are not, however, concerned to demonstrate its funereal character, which is obvious to all the world, but to explore in the music those more obscure characteristics which reveal the contrast between Chopin's image of the experience here contemplated, and Beethoven's. The difference will be found striking.

The rhythm is here marked at every beat — compare the persistently unmarked second beat (reading the time as 4-8) of the Beethoven march — and offers but a single instant of relief (the 16th) from the monotony of its four leaden steps. There is hardly a hint of melodic design in the first two bars, so that the rhythmic pattern dominates our consciousness before the sharper melodic definition of feeling is allowed to occur. But when this melody does appear it is given shape by this same reiteration. The laborious melodic ascent of the minor third which we noted in the Beethoven march appears here also; but its sense is notably different. For that ascent now occurs, wearily, at the weak fourth beat of the measure, so that the normal rhythmic strength of the following first beat is weakened by the already half-accomplished descent. This weaker C then falls to a succession of B♭'s whose dwindling vitality suffers complete exhaus-

---

* Beethoven, like Bach, was too sensitive to the intrinsic meaning-value of this chord to be led, like many a later nineteenth-century composer, into over-use of its seductive sensuous appeal.

Ex. 7

tion at the third beat of the bar. The superficial motion-impression — perhaps because of the regularity of its marking — here suggests, even more than in the Beethoven, the physical reality of slow, measured treading; but the implication of energy is vastly different.

The lack of rhythmic variety is greatly enhanced by the even greater monotony of the harmony. In all the first fourteen bars there are only two chords. These, however, stand in a singular relation of instability to each other. The first is the tonic minor; the second is a major triad (the sub-mediant 6-4), taken by skip (Bb to Db) in the bass. Progression by skip to a second inversion usually has a strong tendency to suggest a change of key, making the root of the 6-4 chord (here, Gb) the tonic of the new key. But this change does not here occur, so that there is a continual sense of stress in the heavy swing, back and forth, between the two chords. The note B♭, common to the two chords and also conspicuous in the melody, has thus two different values — that of tonic rest tone and then (because of the suggestion of G♭ as possible tonic) a much less firm quality as "third" of the unstable G♭ chord. Since this weaker harmonic value always appears on the rhythmically weak beat of the bar, the recurrent B♭'s thus convey a sense of pressure, release, and pressure; and the effect of this repetitive alternation, added to the monotony of the rhythm, is singularly cumulative. These values are then intensified in the ensuing repetition of the first melodic phrase a third higher (with the original melodic line still present as "alto"). Here the accented, active E♭, added to what was before a single and active C, is much more suggestive of pain than was the C alone.

Following this a second melodic phrase appears, only one bar in length and more incisive in its sweeping, downward curve. Its rhythmic design, however, is nearly identical * with that of the second bar of the first melodic phrase, and structural symmetry (as well as apparent expressive purpose) demands its immediate repetition, so that the characteristic and monotonous insistence on a single type of impression is in no way relieved. In this phrase, also, the moments of dynamic intensity and pitch coincide on the first note, so that the melody thereafter wails downward into exhaustion on the unstable 6-4 chord while the blind monotony of mood is maintained by the ever-present two-chord formula of the harmony. No power of resistance to the encompassing gloom is anywhere in evidence. The vicious circle of self-excited feeling grows in the ensuing terrible crescendo to a point of something like hypnotic suggestion.

But at the peak of this curve this disaster — for a moment at least — is averted. With a clear harmonic turn, extraordinarily decisive in its shaking off of the persistent figures so far heard, the major key of D♭ appears, and a strong, upward-tending phrase, accompanied by a tender antiphonal pendant, gives relief from the now almost intolerable burden of self-centered grief. The immediate repetition of this strain, however, is darker and lower (in the original key of B♭ minor), so that its inconclusive ending, its continuance in weaker and weaker rumblings of drum-like trills under an almost obscured melodic line, and the final resumption of the

---

*In some editions it is precisely identical, the B♭ being a dotted 8th and the A♭ a 16th. (The reading given in our illustration appears to be preferable.)

original two-chord rhythm, all serve to establish ineluctably the sense of intolerable and fearsome depression.

Our analysis of this music has been conducted with a much less careful discrimination of the individual elements than was used in examining the Beethoven march. The fusion of the values of stress and motion is here so complete that they could be separately exhibited only with laborious effort and a corresponding blurring of the expressive point at issue. But enough has been said to show that this music is almost maniacal. Its appealing sonorous substance, presenting tensions of easily endurable harshness, provides, for the hearer who will not probe beneath its surface, no more than an agreeable bath in the luxury of vicarious woe. Beneath that surface there is visible the soul of a man to whom death is but darkness and horror. But where could one find, in poetry or any other art, a truer revelation than Beethoven gives of the heroic mind, confronting unafraid the somber fact of earthly finality?

Such discrimination of character as this cannot be made if music is regarded as valuable for its musical interest alone. For the artistry with which the two "purely" musical concepts are realized is at least nearly equal. In each the material is flawlessly handled; in each convincing musical vividness is attained. But these pieces are significant not merely in their exhibition of artistic skill, but in their revelation of pregnant emotional character. If the Beethoven march be accounted the greater it is not because of his superior skill as musician, but because of his ability to reflect, through the medium of music, experience that is in itself neither musical nor in any immediate way aesthetic. The question "Was the work worth doing?" takes, in this light, precedence over the other two, and appears as indeed the final question for artistic criticism.

There is probably no one who would presume to offer a final measure of worth, even for "pure" music. Still less would one set up fixed criteria of value where vital experience is in question. Most of us, however, will agree that he who sees death as a mere misery of extinction is of lesser stature than he who sees it as conjoined with the larger scheme of life; and he who for the moment endows us with his own wider vision is greater than he whose frail violence makes us weep for him and for ourselves.

MUSIC OF VERBALLY UNKNOWN CONTENT

The expressive meaning of the last two examples may well have appeared so obvious as to require no demonstration. Our concern, however, was not merely to show that the obvious and also the more hidden meaning was resident in the music, but to show where that meaning resided and how it was conveyed through the elements and accessories of musical expression as we are trying to understand them. A debatable process, directed toward the attainment of a known end, is more easily expounded than one directed toward an unknown end. Ultimately, however, that process must attain the unknown end; and it is now time to attempt the analysis of music to whose expressive purpose no external clue exists.

Hitherto also, our analysis has been open to the objection that it dealt with fragments only and not with whole compositions. It has been necessary, too, to magnify greatly the detail that we have observed, so that almost microscopic suggestion has been made to appear more significant than, in the normal course of listening experience, it could ever be. Yet, under our microscope, these values do appear; and like the once-perceived etymologies of words, they contribute incalculably to that awareness of meaning which is formed during — or after — a normal experience of hearing or study. But the full significance of musical ideas is not ordinarily conveyed by single thematic utterances such as we have thus far mostly considered. We must therefore rectify the perspective of our whole process of expression, as that process has so far been set forth, if it is to be seen as operative under the normal conditions of musical presentation. It may be well to preview the principal results of such a rectification.

The emergence of a theme as the compact, often epigrammatic core of a musical discourse is the product of a long historic evolution — far too long for review here. Its gradual emergence, however, dictated the general rhetorical pattern of all later musical utterance. For it gave the possibility, in musical discourse, of that intelligible beginning, middle, and end which Aristotle (anticipating and summarizing all later rhetorical elaboration) laid down as the only rational plan for the organization of a discourse.

The essential brevity of the well-conceived theme is, however, too great for the conveyance of all its implications; and some manner of thematic repetition became, accordingly, the only process through which those implications could be revealed. Merely literal repetition, of course, could hardly be more endured in music than in speech. Hence the repetitions must be so varied, and yet so related to each other, as to form a design, and that design must be both logically and aesthetically satisfying. Logical coherence and aesthetic interest may be attained without involving any extraneous expressive purpose, and structural irrelevance, which must appear as aesthetic incongruity, will be repellent.

But if the composer's purpose be at the same time expressive, a more complex problem of relevancy and of aesthetic congruity confronts him. If new thematic matter is required (as it may well be) for continuation of a discourse, the new matter must be compatible with the older not only in musical substance and design but in expressive meaning; and this relevancy is not easy to attain. Faultless writing — assuming that to be faultless which is both complete in its structural logic and coherent in its expressive interest — is rare enough in literature as well as in music. Our present analytical problem will be difficult enough without our having to dispose of irrelevancies. We shall take, therefore, a faultless example, hoping, through consideration of its whole design as well as of its detail, to rectify the distortions due to our earlier magnification of detail and so to put the whole fact of expression into truer perspective.

That example is the great fugue in C-sharp minor from the first book of the *Well-tempered Clavichord*. It has no other title than *Fuga IV*, which indicates nothing beyond its structural form (and not all of that, for the reader is left to discover for himself that this is a "triple" fugue — one with three themes or subjects).* To the general mind the fugal form is assumed to be the most purely musical of all the extant patterns of musical art. Bach gave not one single hint of his expressive purpose, even in those conventional directions for tempo and dynamics which later composers provide, and which have been copiously added to his scores by modern editors. Neither is there any authoritative "interpretation" to be found, although Czerny (deriving his notions from hearing Beethoven perform the music) and editors like Riemann and Busoni have offered fairly extended comment of an interpretative nature. These comments, indeed, bear internal evidence of having been derived through that same intuitive insight which we are attempting to justify; but they were derived from the music itself, which must be our only source, and we shall ignore them in our discussion. Our problem will be not only to see what the various thematic ideas contain, in themselves, of expressive sense, but to judge

---

* The over-erudite reader may also discover the essential features of the second and third themes in the texture of the exposition of the first (the second theme in the bass, bars 17 and 18, and the third, more obscurely, in the bass at bars 4 and 5 and elsewhere); but such root-grubbing yields no insight into Bach's clear and logical musical thought. This piece was intended to be heard as a triple, not a simple, Fugue.

of the meaning of the whole work as we shall see it in retrospect when its expressive and structural details (which are not unrelated) have been fused into that single awareness which the composer intended to evoke.

Ex. 8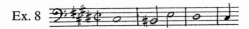

In the pregnant first subject of this fugue (Ex. 8) we find a type of motion less kinetic, more intrinsically impeded, and directed toward a more obscure goal, than in any other theme we have considered. The heaviness of the Beethoven theme was mitigated by rhythmic energies both within itself and in its accompaniment; but this theme "drags its slow length along" with neither any sensible rhythmic propulsion nor any apparent aim for its motive effort. The ground of this heaviness is thus to be sought in the peculiar stress relations of the notes. We shall therefore abandon our former plan of considering the contributions of each element of expression separately and observe (as we must in the normal process of hearing) whatever seems to contribute to the immediate expressive sense.

We shall naturally (and rightly) assume the long initial C♯ to be the tonic. Its length and its low register, as well as the certainly implied *pianissimo* of its utterance,* give it weight, solemnity, even mystery. The long C♯ moves at last downward to B♯ (in itself a hint of weight in the

---

* This statement alone (and far more those which follow) will cause much elevation of the eyebrows among the students of *Aufführungspraxis*. Their conscientious effort to reconstruct the conditions of performance of the music of Bach's day — in particular, the restriction of dynamic contrasts to the stark opposition of *piano* and *forte* — will apparently be set at naught, and that bane of all such serious students, the "romantic" manner of musical utterance, will appear to be recommended.

With some reservation, this criticism must be accepted as just. We question, quite frankly, the probability that a performance of this fugue (and still more of great dramatic scenes such as arise in the second part of the St. John's passion) according merely to the literal prescriptions of *Aufführungspraxis* would have met with the approval of the man who imagined this music. For the end result of such performances as this is not the immediate communication (such as was accomplished by the performance of our Bach concerto) of a musical idea still alive after two hundred years. It is only a history lesson, as indisputable — and as deficient in vitality — as a doctor's thesis. And Bach was not a musicologist.

In the light of our study, it will appear that he wrote the language of music somewhat as his contemporaries, the translators of the King James version of the Bible, wrote English — with imaginative insight into the language not only as a structure but as a vehicle for the communication of ideas beyond the realm of structure. In their preoccupation with structure the musicologists sometimes forget this. In their preoccupation with the prescriptions of the musicologists, their not too percipient pupils forget to load their vehicle with its proper burden and offer performances which sound like the rattle of an empty cart.

C♯) which note, for the same reason, still moves slowly although its activity as leading-tone is manifest. But this B♯ now rises to E; and the interval of a diminished fourth *makes active* this E, which is normally a rest-tone. The implicit contractile tendency of the diminished fourth compels the descent to D♯; but this note is also active, and by its greater length and by its position on the strong beat of a strong measure (the rhythm is dactylic, and D♯ begins a second foot which will appear as spondaic) it receives the major rhetorical emphasis of the whole phrase. The whole impression of motion is thus extremely laborious, and this fact is the more conspicuous because the final rest-tone, C♯, is hardly allowed to convey the expected sense of rest. For at this instant the "answer" (the subject in another voice) enters on the G♯ above, attracting our attention to this voice and submerging the conclusion of the original subject.

So much of motion and tension is indisputable musical fact. Magnification was perhaps necessary in order to make it visible; but these things, to normal vision, are still *there*. They are conveyed by no more than five notes — a compact and epigrammatic reduction of idea to its simplest terms which must command the admiration of any mind aware of the principles of structure.

But there may be more in this design than a feat of structure. The tone-stresses and motions may also portray the tensions and the motor impulses of a mind contemplating other than purely musical experience. And if we ask what, in our own store of emotional experience, corresponds to the suggestions here given, we shall probably agree that such motion implies a heavy spiritual burden; that the tone-stresses are like those of perplexity and doubt; and that together they shadow forth a state of groping anxiety, pervasive and deep-seated, not concerned with trivial things.

If now we follow more rapidly the further course of the exposition of this theme we shall see that its intrinsic sense is amplified in many ways. It is gradually but not greatly intensified by the successive entrances of the subject in higher registers; its inconspicuous countersubject (essentially, four *descending* quarter-notes) imparts no sense of superficial haste, even at the 26th bar where eighth-notes, not quarters, delineate this pattern; but its harmony is persistently dissonant. Discord is almost invariably present at the first beat of the measure, and predominates greatly throughout this whole section of the fugue. Even the brief moments of true concord are almost always harmonized by secondary triads (those whose roots are other than the first, fourth, or fifth notes of the scale); and these triads have a value analogous to active notes in melody. The general intensity of the discord employed is also remarkably level, so that no sharp contrasts appear, and no moments of incisive pain. The activity, however, is unbroken. There is no true cadence until the thirty-fifth bar, and this remarkably long syntactical curve (which by similar devices is even exceeded in length in the Prelude to this fugue) is again a fact of similar character to that suggested by the subject itself.

But that long-delayed cadence, with its sudden brightness as the major tonality at last appears, is singularly apt as preparation for a new theme (Ex. 9). This, from the moment of its introduction, so far permeates the

Ex. 9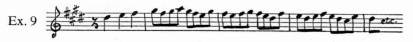

texture of the music that it becomes a factor of high import for the whole impression to be conveyed. It is, however, rather a figure than a theme. It has no rhythmic variety save for the contrast of the initial quarter-notes with the ensuing eighths, and is harmonically only an ornamental progression of descending thirds. But the figure can ascend (its pattern being then inverted) with as great ease as it descends. Its pitch-stresses are in themselves unsuggestive, acquiring significance only through their relation to other voices. It has, in fact, but one outstanding characteristic — a type of motion intrinsically vital (although it is by no means nervous or excited or boisterous) which stands in singularly suggestive relation to the first theme and its whole exposition. It should be noted that the three introductory quarter-notes do not always appear. When they do occur, however, they will be found subtly to augment the vigor of the whole musical fabric, establishing each time a slightly higher plane of intensity which thereafter is never departed from. They appear in bars 44, 51, and 59; in the sequential climb through bars 72–73; in bar 76, and finally in bar 81, where, as we shall see, the purpose of this theme is nearly fulfilled.

In itself, this theme is of little expressive significance. But it is not to be considered merely for itself. At its first appearance it is combined with the first theme, and its purpose is patently to energize, if not that theme, at any rate the almost static tension portrayed by it. It has also another and a more significant purpose — that of preparation and support for another thematic idea of the utmost importance for the whole thought of the composition.

This brief and trenchant idea (Ex. 10) enters at bar 49 in combination with the other two themes. Here, in contrast to the impeded motion of the first theme and the somewhat aimless activity of the second, is motion both decisive and purposeful. There are no subtleties of artificial discord, but only the leap from the least stable to the firmest of rest-tones — from the dominant to the tonic of the key which is now established as F♯ minor. The emphasis of that firmest note is intensified by measured and incisive repetition, at even time-intervals, until the fullest weight is given to the rhythmically strongest note — the downbeat of the second bar of the theme. This note, moreover, is given added force through its discordant harmonization. Although by this device the F♯ is compelled to move to E♯ (the most active note in the key) the tonic sense of F♯ is not lost.* Rather, through the kinetic curve, E♯–D♯–E♯, which dwells on the leading-tone as if it were gathering still more energy, and whose return to the tonic is obscured (as was that of the first theme) by the harmony, we are made to feel a suggestion of insuperable power. Surely, this theme is the very stuff of triumph?

Ex. 10

Added to the already complex web woven (by five voices) out of the first two themes, the full value of this new thought is not at once apparent. Like the first theme, it is a kind of epigram whose compacted meaning requires elucidation. This is amply provided. For at each of those moments of increasing vitality that are marked, as we have seen, by the inclusion of the three prefatory notes of the second theme, the power of this new idea is seen to grow and expand. At last, at bar 94, the energizing second theme has served its full purpose and is dropped from the texture. And now the whole meaning of the third subject in its relation to the first is at last made plain in the series of amazing *stretti* which begin at this point. For, from its dominating position at the top of the musical fabric, the first theme with its doubt and depression is brought lower, in voice after voice, until it reaches the bottom, while at the same time the theme

---

* The F♯ is here so strong that it seems rather to pull the accompanying harmony out of its orbit into discordance with this note than merely to be made discordant by that harmony. This is only another instance of the extreme subtlety and suggestiveness of musical tone-relations. The terms "activity" and "rest" offer but gross and clumsy definition of such value.

of triumph, beginning in the lowest voices, climbs upward in repetition after eager repetition until it achieves a dominance that, even to the eye and without the aid of the ear, represents as overwhelming an insurgence of feeling as was ever uttered.

Yet Bach is not misled by his enthusiasm into a falsification of the real sense of his themes. A close on the note of triumph would have been inappropriate, not to their value as purely musical thoughts, but to their implications as referring to those regions of extramusical experience which seem indubitably to have generated them. In a broadened peroration whose very structure prompts the instinct of the performer to a gradual lessening of intensity, the two opposing themes are combined in a tension which seems to admit that their antagonism is eternal.

Now, assuming that the sense we have read into (or rather, out of) the themes of this composition is supported by our hypothesis of a knowable relation between the substance of music and that awareness of experience which takes, in consciousness, the form of a feeling-attitude toward experience, what is to be our final impression of the whole musical "thing" that has been presented to us? For this thing is possessed of many other interests than that value of expressiveness which has so far engaged our whole attention; and the value of the object as a work of art cannot be assessed in that one light alone.

There is immense interest, certainly, in the music simply as music. Merely as a tonal stimulus it offers the impressive appeal of a careful selection and a controlled arrangement of musical matter, appellant both to the ear and to the mind. This controlled arrangement, however — this musical form — turns out to be a highly complex fact. It obviously obeys familiar principles of organization; but that obedience is no mere slavish docility. Tone and rhythm, the elements of the substance of music, have been employed in a way to which no competent observer can remain indifferent. Seen only as an example of Hanslick's *tönend bewegte Form*, the work has a beginning, a middle, and an end.

But is this all? Or is it possible that this "end" is the conclusion of a discourse which, in itself thoroughly musical, is also more than musical? If expressive sense at all comparable to that which we have found in the themes is actually resident there, it is hardly supposable that the whole form of the work was conceived and executed in indifference to that sense.

We found in the themes suggestions of depression, animation, and confidence — or at any rate of spiritual states which, for lack of more precise

119

and vivid verbal symbols, we call by such names as depression, animation, and confidence. These words suffice merely to symbolize those states in their gross aspect. The themes define them (and hence define the words also) with much of that discrimination for their intrinsic character and intensity with which we observe the states themselves as we undergo them. The whole musical composition presents these suggestions in an arrangement which, seen as purely musical, is orderly and satisfying. But if the constructive effort was indeed purely musical, these suggestions (which in that light would appear as indiscriminate outbursts of disrelated feeling) would have appeared as a hindrance rather than a contribution to constructive effort. Were they a hindrance? Or were they a determinant factor in the organization of the form? These questions cannot be evaded.

If, as we contend, they were not a hindrance but a help — if the representation of some aspect of emotional states was an item in the whole structural problem — then some apprehension of those states must also be an item in our effort to understand the structure. Those states — the products of external experience which, in its factual aspect, music cannot portray — are chiefly intelligible when seen as related to, and in terms of, their causal experience. Awareness of this experience, when only the feeling-resultant of experience is portrayed, must be gained through a kind of inference. But if this awareness, as often happens, takes the not unnatural form of an image of event, then the music will appear, in spite of its incapacity, to portray that event.

Musical themes and their elaborations follow each other in time. These are the actual musical events. Physical events which such a hearer may find portrayed in the music likewise follow each other in time. That hearer will then be naturally inclined to suppose that the order of events in a musical composition is also the order in which his imagined physical events occur.

Such an assumption is quite gratuitous. Music very seldom successfully represents events. But association, drawing from some few suggested data the obvious inferences, erects the emotional characteristics which *are* portrayed into emotional experiences which are promptly translated into successions of physical event; and lo! in the twinkling of an eye that which once was music has become a story.

The danger of indulging in such over-exuberant fancy may be illustrated by allowing this instinct for narrative a moment of liberty with our fugue. The profound character of the first theme may justifiably be interpreted in a religious sense. So taken, it may at once be personified. It will appear, then, no longer an expression of the emotional state of depression, but the portrait of a man who is depressed and yearning for light. Such a man was Christian, in *The Pilgrim's Progress*. The theme then will readily become a kind of leading-motive for Christian, and the exposition of the fugue an account of those spiritual perplexities which impelled him to undertake his journey. The second theme (not without difficulty, for it is hardly turbulent in character, but irrelevance is a minor matter to a mind embarked on adventure) will serve for all the distractions and perils he encounters, from the temptations of Mr. Worldly Wiseman to the battle with Apollyon. And the third (more accommodatingly) will stand for the abiding faith and zeal that leads Christian through the Slough of Despond (which the first theme may now be made to represent, even though we began by giving it a quite different sense) onward and upward to the point where the heavy burden of sin is loosened (see bar 94!) and with a great hymn of reconciliation and praise Christian enters into the glories of the Celestial City. Truly, it is a trivial tale that music tells.

This unwarrantable plot — even less absurd than many another, perpetrated even by composers themselves* — could only be contrived on the assumption that the order of musical event implied a parallel order of physical event. Thematic development would hardly be interesting if it did not attain to points of climax. But there is no reason whatever to interpret the succession here exhibited as a narrative order. It may be, and in music it mostly is, *an arrangement for effectiveness*, whether constructive or expressive, in the detail; and is thus more akin to pictorial than to verbal composition. It appears more reasonable, then, to view the various expressive suggestions and developments offered by this fugue as standing in relations which are rightly to be understood only when the whole piece can be grasped as the portrayal of a single, highly inclusive emotional attitude.

It would also be gratuitous for us to suppose that the attitude here portrayed was suddenly conceived by the composer as a moment of inspira-

* E.g., Bruckner's own "program" for his Fourth (Romantic) Symphony: "A medieval city — morning dawns — from the city's towers awakening calls resound — the gates are opened — on mettled steeds the knights ride out into the open — the magic of the forest surrounds them — forest murmurs — songs of birds — and thus the romantic picture is developed." The listener, if made expectant by prior reading of this very literal description, will find it impossible to discover in the music the tonal suggestions of any of the details of this scene except the opening horn-call.

tion, and is thus a product of that immediate excitement. No more than any other thoughtful artist (and none who is not thoughtful is an artist) does the musical composer merely set down the moods which color his perception as he takes up his pen. A foolish credulity has somehow fostered the notion that music, being the language of the emotions, is therefore the immediate utterance of emotion — of passing fancies, passions, or trances, dashed onto paper in an ecstasy of inspiration — miraculous in origin therefore, and approachable for contemplation only by a mind despoiled, for that moment, of rationality. Why or whence a musical idea arises in a composer's mind is indeed a mystery — almost as much to him as to his naive admirer; but so is the genesis of all creative ideas. That they arise out of experience and thus in some measure reflect that experience is, however, a rational assumption. The purist conceives them to arise and to be formed wholly within that region of the mind (fictitious to the psychologist) which is set apart from the rest of consciousness for musical conception and contemplation.* We are contending that there is no such region, but that musical concepts are palpably relatable to large areas of non-musical experience.

This fugue, then, neither tells a story nor represents Bach's reaction to circumstances existent at the time of its composition.

What, then, does it express? Avoiding the narrative suggestion and the still more stupid notion that music is the unconscious product of momentary inspiration — the Scylla and Charybdis of superficial music appreciation — we have found credible musical allusions to states of mind or conditions of experience feebly describable as groping in mystery; awakening energy; and an apparently ultimate sense of triumph. These are at any rate momentarily acceptable symbols for the three themes out of which the fugue is constructed.

Reduced to these verbal terms, the idea of the composition would be puerile. But — as we have perhaps too often insisted — the music is not defined by these words. It defines them. It enlarges their significance through the awakening of that region of consciousness where bald, factual experience has import. Even though that region is here awakened, however, we are not told what the mystery is whose solution is groped for; what energy of mind or muscle is needful to cope with the problem; nor what the real nature of the victory is. But these hints and inferences of

* Cf. Jules Combarieu (in *Musique, ses lois, son évolution* [E. Flammarion, 1907]): *Il existe une pensée musicale.*

factual experience are not isolated. They are synthesized into a single awareness, both retrospective and immediate — the feeling-tone of mature and pondered experience.

The music does not, indeed, describe that experience. Nevertheless we know its nature — not by our certain failure to describe it, but by the certainty with which we reject words that attempt to describe it and fail. For to the extent to which we know what a thing is not, we know what it is. A man's mind, certainly, is here portrayed in action. But that man is no politician, involved in some wily intrigue of state; he is no general, doubtfully planning battle against superior force. He is no lover upon whom his mistress has frowned, no demagogue, no dictator, no hedonist, no priest; no mere crawler between earth and heaven whom earthly business drives on his tiny diurnal round. Here is the mind of one who seeks in that purposeless whirligig a Purpose.

Out of our own experience, no matter how divergent, this same problem has confronted us. And these tones set forth the mind of that seeker — who is now ourself — more swiftly and with a truer profundity than is possible with the machinery of nouns and verbs.

❧ *IX* ❧

The Functioning of the Elements
in the Sonata Form

THE foregoing has offered a general demonstration of the functioning of our hypothetical elements of expression. That demonstration, involving much detail, has perhaps blurred the somewhat difficult identification of the elements themselves. It has certainly blurred that relation of form to content which, with our illustrative stanza as a basis, we tried to define in the third chapter. It will doubtless have been understood that we intend no disparagement of form, and that we have merely ignored that one value, being preoccupied with another. But if the relation of form to expression is important in poetry, it must be equally important in music. We shall continue our study of the functioning of the elements in a wider field than that covered in our attempt to demonstrate both their existence and their functioning, and shall take more account of form and its relation to expression. But since expression in music is achieved by a process so different from that of language, it may be well to offer a kind of abstract of the expected results of our study before entering upon its detail. For detail, multiplied, may obscure the point it seeks to illustrate.

Although we shall strive for precision, that study (like the preceding) will necessarily lack the exactness of scientific observation. Even the elements of musical structure, as seen in the musician's eye, are not facts as the physicist sees fact. Tone, in its purely physical aspect, is not tone as the musician hears it; rhythm is rather a concept of relation in time and stress than a congeries of facts in these fields; and the physical analysis of harmony yields results so far from explanatory of the musician's harmonic apprehensions as to be all but useless to him in the practice of his art. And even the "fact" of musical form — far more objective than the

124

fact of expression — is too intractable to be measured by the micrometers of the scientist. Form, as we know it, is a concept rather than a positive fact of tone-relation.

The elements of expression, as we have defined them, although based on these supposititious facts of structure, are still less precisely factual. They are a product of those facts; but they are a derivative, not an essential product, and their functional process is still more dependent upon conceptual interpretation of the musical substance than is the process of musical structure. Yet, in the whole perspective of art, musical structure, and, as we think, musical expression also, *are* facts: not isolated and objective, but synthetic and experiential. But in this perspective they raise many questions which we have as yet not attempted to answer.

The most inclusive of these is that of the relation of musical expression to form. In our long observation of the fact of expression we have almost ignored the aesthetic interest of form — an interest which, for the average listener who subsumes the whole question of musical value under his individual definition of beauty, is doubtless paramount. In our earlier study of the relation of form to expression, those two values were observed in poetic guise. Having now attained some notion of the nature and the process of musical expression, we must attempt to define this relation as it is exhibited in music.

We found in our poetic stanza that the primary poetic substance (the word) could appear as both a fact of expression and a fact of form. The definitional meaning of words, however, is so far fundamental for all language that poetic form cannot be wholly isolated from expression. Even the unquestionably decorative devices (rhyme, alliteration, "effective" alterations of syntactical order, etc.) as well as the subtle values of poetic meter (patently akin to our "element" of ideal motion) are unimaginable wholly apart from the primary symbolism of words. The most important function of form in poetry is thus to add an incalculable increment of meaning to definitional verbal sense. And since form thus serves not only for delight and for ornament, but even in this guise contributes to that ability which is human understanding, form is here the servant and expression the master.

Can this be true of music also? The notion, to the musical purist, will seem absurd; but it will at least bear examination.

To be expressive, a communication must convey an idea. We have defined idea as an image and a valuation of experience, and are bound by that definition.* An idea ordinarily originates in a fairly concrete image of confronted experience. That awareness becomes an idea only when the significance of the object is apprehended. Awareness of that significance (the valuation of the image) *forms itself* in the mind of him who confronts the experience — forms itself out of such resources and facilities for association as the observer possesses.

Words, the commonly accepted symbols for facts of experience, are admirably capable of evoking images of experience. Yet the essential fixity of association between the verbal symbol and its object deprives the symbol of that elasticity of reference which may evoke the valuation of that object — the way it appears to *you,* at this instant, in this context.

Those configurations of tonal tension and rhythm which we are calling the elements of expression, and through which music makes its most tangible and significant reference to extramusical experience, are not (as words are) fixed and commonly accepted symbols for fixed and generally familiar items of such experience. They consequently convey little or nothing of that essential image-factor of idea. They do imply, however — rather than symbolize, although their implication may have even more than the vividness of a symbol — the valuation of such an image, especially in its feeling aspect. Their contribution to idea thus resembles, in substance, what we have called the poetic increment of words.

The resemblance is in substance, however, rather than in function. For poetic increment makes words grow in meaning, but does not in itself possess meaning. It is thus an addition to the sense already resident in words. The elements of expression are not an increment of form. It is true that tonal tension and rhythm are factors of purely musical form. But in this aspect they are not elements of expression. They *become* — by those associative accretions we have noted, and which necessitated an enlarged definition of the facts of tonal tension as "tone-stress" and of rhythm as "ideal motion" — elements of expression. Yet, although they derive from and enlarge the interest of form, these are not in any proper sense increments of form. They are increments of interest where music

* Pure musical form appears to the comprehending observer as an image of musical organization and hence, quite properly, of musical "experience." The aroused awareness of a musical form is thus apparently an idea in our sense of that word. But the experience involved is musical experience itself; the image is that of the musical object in its own context and no other; the valuation (including sensuous delight, not intrinsically a value of form) is still exclusively in that context; and the idea generated by pure form is thus an evocation rather than an expression.

is seen as a communication, rather than as simply an evocation, of idea; and form itself — an essential of music but not its essence — remains, in the expressive musical fabric, the servant of expressive purpose, not its master.

This should serve to establish a general theorem of the relation of form to meaning in music. The specific proportions of these components and their relative significance must obviously be determined for any individual work. But another question will immediately arise. Since tonal stress and rhythm appear in all music, must all music be regarded as tentatively expressive? Or is there a kind of threshold of expressive intimation below which these primarily formal components of the musical substance remain only formal? If so, where does that threshold lie? Does it lie higher — i.e., is form itself in music to be accounted more significant — than in the other arts? And again, above that threshold, are contradictions of actually expressive suggestion possible within a single, *structurally acceptable* musical form — contradictions so confusing to the perception of meaning that no coherent *expressive* sense can be found in the work?

All these questions will be seen to involve, in a degree hitherto unconsidered in our study, the relation of form to expression. Categorical answers are hardly possible. But instances in which the conditions in question arise may be observed, and tolerable answers, probably valid for similar conditions, may be found. We were able to evade these questions in our study of the C-sharp minor fugue; for while the logic of that work — and of the fugal form in general — is indisputable, the themes themselves were so meaningful that the whole structural organization, in the light of that meaning, appeared as the perfect vehicle for the really creative idea of the piece. But the expressive range of the fugal form, ordinarily based on a single theme, is contracted by that limitation;* and a form of wider expressive horizon will give a clearer and more rapid view of the questions at issue.

The Sonata, being polythematic and homophonic, is such a form. We shall present several examples, selected to illustrate some of the ques-

---

* The range is contracted, but not the depth. Compare with our example the simple (monothematic) fugues in D♯ minor (No. VIII), in F minor (No. XII), in G♯ minor (No. XVIII), in B♭ minor (No. XXII), and in B minor (No. XXIV) in the first book of the *Well-tempered Clavichord*. The close approach to actual drama, present in our example and in large measure owing to the fact that this was a triple fugue, is of course missing (the "master-stretto" in the B♭ minor is electrifying, but in a cumulative, not a dramatic sense); but the experience contemplated in each, while patently different from that of the C♯ minor, is of comparable profundity.

tions just posed. The first will be from Mozart, where formal perfection is indisputable, but where the threshold of expression is less easy to locate. This is the Sonata in F (K. 332).

It begins with a buoyant melodic line:

Ex. 11

which shows, at the third bar, a relatively high degree of tension. The upward leap, after four rest-tones, is from active note to active; harmonic progression is almost out of the tonic key; the swaying motion, pursuing the same pattern for three bars, makes its active-note leap with utter ease; and the little twitch before the pause seems to suggest a continuation in the same vein. But the next strain:

Ex. 12

not only does not continue this buoyancy; it almost contradicts it. Angular, generally descending motion, rest-tone emphasis, and a cadential halt with every two-bar phrase except the third — all these things, if they do not contradict, at least abandon the fluidity so promisingly portrayed in the opening. It is as if the image of experience, whose valuation this opening portrays, had suddenly faded; or as if the melodic invention, momentarily vivid, had failed, and a perfunctory consequent had been allowed to complete an antecedent whose implications had not been wholly realized. It is true that the initial impression is vivid enough to color the rather lame conclusion, so that the loss of character is not sharply apparent; but the whole creative impulse appears to have been too swift to allow of any pause for the effortful designing of more consistent character.* This is seen in the immediate continuation:

* Compare, in this respect, the opening of the *Allegro* of the E♭ Symphony (No.

Ex. 13

which — since the really high suggestion of the opening phrase has now become diffused — nonchalantly substitutes a much flimsier but still delightful dance-step for the more deeply animated motion of the beginning.

Delicate ornamentation of the dotted up-beat figures of this phrase, together with two dainty reiterations of cadential harmony, complete the thought. Then comes a sudden relatively violent transition to D minor, at first energetic in motion and then stressful in its emphasis of the diminished seventh chord:

Ex. 14

Since the first two bars show an over-all rise on D–F–A, the arpeggio of the tonic chord, a structural resemblance may be detected between this figure and that of the opening of the sonata; but this new phrase is so different in rhythmic pattern and in total emphasis that the similarity is neither structurally nor expressively significant.

The contrast, of course, was necessary. The essence of the sonata form lies in its presentation of contrasting ideas — sometimes highly antithetical, sometimes more subtly opposed. In general, the antithesis appears as that between vigor and gentleness, and in a large majority of sonata forms vigor makes the first appeal to the attention, with gentleness emerging out of dwindling vigor. In this work that usual procedure (for perfectly sound reasons) is departed from. Gentleness is primary for the character of the whole movement; vigor is secondary; and vigor thus appears as episodic. The episode is long and, in the whole harmonic con-

39). Its principal theme has a buoyancy not unlike that of the opening of this sonata; but here the image does not fade, and the whole thought retains its character.

129

text, highly modulatory. Neither does it dwindle in preparation for the true second subject; but its emphatic close gives sharpness of definition to the second theme, and this is of considerable value, for that theme,

Ex. 15

emerging out of the strongly suggested C minor key in the unexpected brightness of C major, gains much in the definition of its character by that fact of surprise. Like the dance-motive that concluded the first sub-ject-group, this is delicately ornamented; it is even akin to that phrase in character; but in consequence the essential antithesis appears, not be-tween the first and second subjects, but between those and the episodes. For what follows is another long episode, beginning in a certain lyrical sonority but eventuating in rhythmic and harmonic ejaculation, whose actually episodic relation to the whole design is shown by the brief return to the second theme (considerably altered) before the needful but per-functory closing figures bring the long and diffuse exposition to an end. The second long episode furnishes the substance of the brief develop-ment section.

It is inconceivable that such contrasts of character and such general looseness of design as this movement exhibits could have been the product of any sharply defined expressive purpose. If the various features are ex-amined in the perspective of expression which we believe our elements to provide, many hints of definite and even interesting feeling experience may be found; but in the perspective of normal listening it is evident that the music lies only occasionally above the threshold of expressive in-terest.*

---

* Our discussion of this piece (and those to follow) will doubtless appear to imply that in our opinion music which lies below the threshold of expressive inter-est is of relatively little value, and that value grows in proportion as interest rises above that level. This, as a general proposition, can hardly be denied. Profound thought *is* more significant than triviality. But our very competence to judge of profundity derives from extended contact with the relatively trivial; every experi-ence takes on more or less of significance according to its context; and these con-texts of experience — in general, the amenities of civilized life — yield a finely ad-justed matrix of form (or convention) within whose persistently demanded agree-ableness the discrimination of profundity is obscured.

Form, in consequence, is a high value. How far it can really exist, in itself and apart from the intimations of meaning resident in the matrix, is debatable; but when it is conjoined with discriminable profundity it unquestionably rises in value. Yet it will still appear that form, even in its most agreeable aspect, is the handmaiden of meaning.

The Elements in the Sonata Form

In our next example — the Sonata in A (K. 331), written much about the same time as the Sonata in F — Mozart substituted for the usual first-movement form a Theme and Variations. This form will have considerable interest in our present study of the relation of form to expression. It offers the most valuable exercise in musical ingenuity that can be set for students of composition, for that art, beyond its rudiments, is very considerably a problem of development, and development, in the last analysis, is variation. In the development-section of a sonata form, the process is so free as to be without rule. But where a theme is taken (as here) for repeated presentation in varied form, the composer is bound to follow intelligibly the contour of his theme, and the pattern of his work is therefore largely predetermined.

Musical variation is thus very definitely a problem of form. It is also, however, a problem of expression; for if the variations presented no more to the listener than successive repetitions of the single thought contained in the theme, the merely decorative interest of successive alterations of its surface would soon lapse. Each variation, therefore, presents not only the formal outline of the theme but a distinctive character. There is probably no rule that would forbid the inclusion of any purely formal variant of the theme in a set of variations; but there is a very perceptible principle — far more a principle of expression than of form — that will demand relativity of character not only in successive variations but in the whole set.*

Mozart's theme is very slender, naive, and sunny (Ex. 16). To quote it further than we do here is needless; to analyze it would seem an impertinence. Slight as its substance is, it sets an immediately perceptible

---

* The musical variation-form has hardly a parallel in any other art, unless in the dance. Variations of *motive* occur, to be sure, in painting and architecture; but the motive thus varied by no means stands as the foundation of the whole composition, and the variations are thus variations of detail, not of the central theme of the art work. Neither is the variation process natural in language; for language is primarily symbolic of things and acts; even an apparently abstract "theme," in language, implies that congeries of things and acts which we call an event; and to rehearse the same event in the varied guises in which a musical theme may appear would almost inevitably be tedious and repellent. Such a literary composition as Browning's *The Ring and the Book* is indeed a close parallel to the variation form, for the theme — the brutal murder of Pompilia — recurs in every "variation." But that theme remains itself throughout; only its aspect, in the divergent vision of participants or spectators, is varied. The musical theme, however, portrays not event itself but reaction to event; and it may thus yield variations which imply — as did the variants of the figure in our Brünnhilde theme — essentially new experience, involving something of the primary feeling-character but otherwise quite differently oriented.

131

norm of tension — or rather, of release from tension — from which no far departure in the variations would be tolerable. But this norm is well above the threshold of expressive interest. It reflects, perhaps, no more than a state of complete well-being; but that state has a patrician background, for such grace as this is not of common origin. Neither is it wholly self-centered, like Debussy's *Fille aux cheveux de lin*; for the third variation, in A minor, is aware, not indifferently, of pain. Accustomed as

we are to intensities of utterance which would have sounded brutal to Mozart and his audiences, we may fail to catch the gentle implication. For the mere lapse into the minor key was a descent of considerable import for eighteenth-century ears, and the whole design has accordant implications. The tripping motion of the thematic line becomes undulant; its point of rhetorical emphasis is shifted from the fourth beat of the measure to the fifth; and that point is attained through the contractile interval of the diminished third (D$\sharp$–F$\natural$). The ensuing repetition in octaves, in consequence of the subtlety of this line, is singularly forceful, and in no merely brilliant sense. The beginning of the second section, with its leap of the octave, intensifies the undulant figure of the opening and reaches, in the slightly declamatory emphasis of its return to the recapitulation, as high a degree of tension as the established norm would allow. And the measure of this tension is revealed in the exquisite release from it which appears with the next variation.*

The foregoing illustrations have been advisedly chosen from Mozart's earlier (pre-Viennese) works. Expressive purpose is here secondary to the pursuit of what his age would have described as beauty — a creation in which the primary value was the sheer delight in tonal form. But to rouse the "affections" was also an objective;† and our two illustrations have

---

* Quite another measure of the perfect continence of Mozart's work may be found in Reger's gargantuan Variations and Fugue on this same theme. In comparison to their thematic source his complexities have that excess in both form and expression which we noted in our quotation from Swinburne. Mozart might indeed have admired the ingenuity of this piece, but he would have shuddered at its taste.

† Mozart's own words often testify to this — e.g., his letter to his father (Sept. 26, 1781) regarding *Die Entführung aus dem Serail*, and especially Belmont's aria, *O wie ängstlich*.

been selected because their expressive values nowadays appear to be considerably submerged in the delightful tonal texture and have to be sought out. Yet, if our thesis of expression holds, they are not only there but can be located. It will considerably substantiate our conclusions so far to examine a later example of Mozart's sonata structure — one in which the threshold of expressive interest is so far crossed that the structural pattern, while it follows without deviation the conventional formal outline, is guided at every turn by expressive purpose.

This is the famous Sonata in C minor (K. 475) with its introductory Fantasia. (They were composed separately but, because of their patent kinship, published together.) Our present study being concerned with the sonata form, our analysis will deal only with the first movement of the sonata. (If merely objective presentation of the fact of expression were our purpose, the Fantasia would appear a still more vivid illustration; but we are now engaged, not merely with the fact of expression but with its relation to the fact of form.) Seen in its structural aspect, the principal theme (Ex. 17) presents, in its first three bars, that conventional arpeg-

Ex. 17

giation of the tonic chord which establishes in the hearer's mind the key of the piece. More than this, however, will be seen if an expressive purpose is sought for. The first motive of two bars contains only rest-tones, whose intrinsic stress lies in their swift ascent; but the motion-pattern is both decisive (in its purposeful on-beat stride) and nervous (in its abrupt, almost breathless "feminine" ending). The second motive, still on rest-tones but with the interval of the descending fifth strongly propelled by the "fidget" of the preceding trill, repeats its downward motion on the active interval of the diminished seventh and again pauses abruptly on a less feminine but still breathless ending. Bars 5–8 form the obvious rhetorical "consequent" of this clause, opposing activity to rest and rest to activity with complete symmetry, and maintaining thus the established tension to the very end of the sentence.

In the ensuing strain (Ex. 18) there is high illumination of the already sharply defined feeling-character. (Compare the patent disrelation of the component phrases in the first subject-group of the F major sonata.) The explosive G; the immediate dynamic contrast; the downward drag of the syncopated upper voice with its chromatic associate; the immediate inversion of these two voices with the chromatic phrases now predominant; the maintenance of the explosive accent at the (still feminine) end of the phrase; and the obstinate drumming of the pedal note G — all these details coalesce toward a portrayal of tension readily relatable to that of our own consciousness when under severe strain. These details are also, indeed, facts of structure; but to observe them in that light only is hardly to enhance their interest.

Ex. 18

It is rational, then, to see these tones as portraying a valuation of experience — the emotional result of exposure to an experience definable with certainty as not happy. The experience is still further negatively discriminable as, for example, *not* of the contemplative and considerably religious order portrayed in our Bach fugue; and *not* of the order of Isolde's dying ecstasy. These are not the nervous tensions and the motor impulses characteristic of those states.

We shall not, it is true, arrive by this process of exclusion at any positive identification — any certain image — of that experience whose valuation is here portrayed. For these perturbations are not only the composer's but our own. And since they are thus familiar, we are certain, not only that they do not arise out of nothing, but that their like has been *in us* the product of many varied concatenations of event. One of these, in our experience, was as provocative as the other. No specific concatenation need therefore be imaged to complete that idea of experience which this music conveys. We must not suppose that any actual experience of our own, no matter how appropriately causative of these perturbations it may appear, was undergone by the composer and became the actual determinant of the musical utterance.*

* Compare, in this light, Mr. Kirkpatrick's remark (quoted on p. 89) on the definiteness of his own imagery of experience as awakened by Scarlatti's sonatas. As a verbal "interpretation" of the music it was palpably insufficient. But as a contribution to his musical interpretation — as a determinant, for him, of the inner sense of the notes — it evidently has incalculable value.

The Elements in the Sonata Form

At the time when this piece was composed (1784), the sonata, as a musical form, was approaching perfection. The loose aggregation of agreeably contrasted thematic fragments, rhythms, and ornaments found in K. P. E. Bach was becoming a closely knit structure, and the essential principle of that structure — in contrast to that which had long been acknowledged as governing polyphony — was the opposition of two co-ordinate themes. Their co-ordinateness being established, subordinate matter in the shape of figures, ornamental passages, or even themes, interjected as transitions between the themes or for rhetorical conclusions, might be introduced. All this, of course, might be seen as a problem of structure — a largely aesthetic discrimination determining the contours and the contrasts. Such, it seems to us, was the principle observed in the creation of the F major sonata.

The C minor sonata exhibits these same structural features. But it also shows signs of ferment in quite another than the purely aesthetic and structural regions of the mind. Emotion is here excited, as it was in the F major; but it is at the same time portrayed. And the creative purpose, thus expanded, not only yields the cogent substance we have so far examined, it governs the whole movement (and indeed — if more loosely — the whole sonata).*

The expressive interest of Example 18 as complement to the opening theme is high. But that this is actually a complement to and an illumination of that theme is seen in the brief return thereafter of the opening phrases — not as the recall of something possibly forgotten, but as the indubitable conclusion of the exordium. And the function of the ensuing strain (Ex. 19) is to release the tension so far maintained in preparation for that contrast in subject-matter which is the distinctive feature of the sonata form. This sub-theme is already in the relative major key in which

* It governs also, and with a more cogent purpose still, the first movement of the G minor Symphony (No. 40). The tiny rhythmic figure out of which the main theme is contrived may, of course, be seen as a structural motive only. So observed (with, of course, concurrent recognition of its tonal appeal) the interest of the music is great. But if — as appears to us rational — that motive is seen as generated out of an experience not in itself musical: an experience akin to that which we are discovering in the C minor sonata, the reiterations take on an insistence hardly less pointed than that of the famous motive in Beethoven's C minor symphony.

Such a vision of the music seems to us to enhance, rather than minimize, the interest of the structure. It is true that structure does recede, so long as the expressive purpose remains in the foreground of attention; but it returns, when seen as conjoined with that purpose, in a juster perspective. And the vision which cannot or will not attain that perspective seems to us frankly myopic.

135

the second theme proper is to occur. But it also partakes of the character of the opening, for its motion-pattern is less new than, in its legato character, it at first appears. Omit the turn and the 8th-note G in the second

Ex. 19

bar and you have precisely the rhythm-pattern of the main theme. These alterations in melodic direction and in motor impulse yield a quite new expressive sense, anticipating the more tranquil second theme; and a more adequate solution of the difficult problem of transition would be hard to imagine. Everything is in character, even the by no means perfunctory chords out of which the hesitant approach to the second theme emerges. In that theme (Ex. 20), the motion-*pattern* of the main theme is again present. Omit the two 16th-notes, shorten the E♮ to a quarter-note, and you have it, precisely. But while this resemblance cannot have been wholly accidental,* the motor-*impulse* which, as a component of emotional ex-

Ex. 20

citement, we had to define by the clumsy term ideal motion, is quite different. The propulsion imparted to the transitional theme (by the swift 32nds and by the two active notes whose rising direction is continued by the hasty 8th-notes to the culminant B♭) is now lessened by the narrow compass of the new theme and its slower rise to the F. The feminine ending (all but obliterated in the transitional theme by the length and emphasis of the B♭) is here given a clinging rather than a driving character. If (as the mere mechanics of structure might have dictated) this phrase had been immediately repeated a tone higher, the release from the earlier tension would have appeared a lapse into indiffernce. But the "answer" to this suggestion is a pregnant strain in the tenor which imparts to the higher voice an implication of weight which that phrase, in itself, hardly

* It is not, however, credible that Mozart calculated in advance, and out of absorption in the problem of musical structure, the rhythmic identities we have just noted. Patently, his awareness of character both generated and controlled his "translation" of that awareness into tone. Such absorption is by no means uncommon. Beethoven's "C-minor motive" occurs in several contemporary compositions: e.g., intact, and with a similar meaning-value in the *Appassionata*; tranquillized into 4-4 time and elevated into an almost unique serenity in the Violin Concerto.

possessed; and the whole theme, in consequence, finds a conclusion wholly appropriate to the whole sense of the music thus far in the accompanying example (Ex. 21), which may be seen as the reduplicated feminine ending,

Ex. 21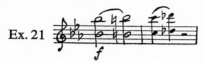

at first broadened, then diminished, and presented in the tensest tonal progressions that could with any propriety have been admitted into this tonal fabric — the rising minor second, progressing from concord to discord.

There is no need to analyse further. It is incredible that this music should have been written without some coherent and governing expressive purpose in mind. An attempt to verbalize that purpose would involve the fictional concoction of some specific circumstance as the image of experience of which the music represents only the valuation. But that valuation, as the music portrays it, is evidence that non-musical experience — too comprehensive to be "typed" by any specific event — was the prime generator of the music.

The perfecting of the so-called "Viennese classical sonata" was thus not a perfecting of form alone. So much seems to us incontrovertibly indicated in our examination of but a few of Mozart's efforts. If we had space to study (omitting Haydn and his lesser contemporaries) even a half dozen of the Beethoven sonatas (and of course the symphonies and chamberworks) we should find, perceptibly from the very beginning but palpably from the end of his first period on, such diversity of character and so just a valuation of implied experience as would make an accounting for these works on a purely stylistic basis quite impossible.

It is doubtless perilous to attempt to amplify that account on the basis of such images of experience as can be derived, by our process of observation, from these works. But it is definitely more dangerous to assume, in the search for a competent critical estimate of them, that a purely stylistic analysis — so "objective" as to be quite impersonal and therefore indisputably truthful for him who has the necessary prior training in the method — can yield such an estimate.*

* It does not appear to strike the mind so trained that such a process of analysis — indubitably acute in observation and earnest in application — has formed itself by precisely the method of observation it now pursues, and that the conclusions at

Our process yields — and to other students than the writer — endless illuminations of the creative effort embodied in the fascinatingly diverse structures comprised in our literature. That extramusical imagery contributed to Beethoven's works is evidenced not so much by such titles as "The Song of Thanksgiving of a Convalescent" — or even by such explanatory phrases (actually associated with the purely instrumental notes but pregnant with implications far beyond this immediate context) as "*Lebe wohl*" or "*Muss es sein? Es muss sein*" — as by the tonal stuff itself. To show this we shall take, as the single example possible within our space, Beethoven's piano sonata in A, Op. 101. Portions only, chosen from two of the four movements, can be considered; and even here a lamentable number of words must be used for the indication of musical ideas communicated in extraordinarily few notes. The opening of the first movement, which will be discussed as briefly as possible, will be found for reference on the opposite page.

Such gentleness as is expressed in the opening phrases of this movement is hardly to be found in musical literature earlier than this. That quality, as a general aspect of the music, is readily recognizable; but the subtlety of it, although it is an actual product of the motions and stresses, may well appear to be hidden rather than revealed by our clumsy, literal description of those facts.

The melody begins on the leading-tone and has active notes on the beat almost throughout the first six measures (both E and A are made active by their unstable harmony). Yet, aside from the one easy leap of an octave, the melodic line never skips by a wider interval than the minor third, and the gentleness we spoke of is in no small measure imparted by the virtually unbroken conjunctness of the melodic line. Its motion, however, is equally contributory. Not a single 16th-note mars its suavity, nor is any external propulsion evident beyond the gently undulant triplet figure which flows and pauses with the melodic line. Neither is there any

which it arrives are in consequence to a certain extent predetermined. It is a curious fact that the sonata form, whose scope of interest (based on thematic antithesis) is greater than that of any earlier form, has not proved readily amenable to "purely" stylistic analysis and remains musicologically unaccounted for.

Beethoven is credibly reported to have remarked that if the world could but understand and act upon the content of his music there would be no more war. It is unlikely that such a remark would have been made by a man whose whole soul was given to the solution of problems of structure *per se*. And it is even more unlikely that the limitless scope of Beethoven's imaginative vision can be revealed by a critical method which by implication would confine that vision to the field of tonal structure only.

Ex. 22

139

sudden or spasmodic discord, although the harmony is almost always active.

The following passage (bars 7–10) is a quiet intensification of the opening thought, with the subtle difference that, in its now undeviating ascent, rest tones, rather than active, appear on the strong beats until the summit of the curve is almost reached (bar 9). Here the B♯, suspended, performs its resolution ornamentally by leaping to D♯ and then returning to the C♯. This progression, unfortunately, is very hard to play with full realization of the "pull" of B♯ to D♯ against the A major chord; for the sonority of the B♯, at the tie, cannot be made audible against the new A major chord without attacking that B♯ more forcefully than is appropriate to the whole melodic curve. Yet it is precisely at this point that that curve takes a new turn, involving the first leap larger than the third — that from C♯ down to F♯; and the just inflection of this peak of the whole melodic curve is of high import for all that follows. For from this peak the whole melodic trend is now downward, with the leap of a fourth, preceded by this same undulance, now characteristic. Observe that all that is included in our quotation forms but one long periodic sentence, the figure after the deceptive cadence (bar 16) being formed after the pattern of bars 10–11, and the actual approach to the E major chord (the new tonic) being delayed to extend the established mood to all rational length. And that which follows (beyond our quotation) preserves the atmosphere of that mood, through the quiet insistence of the cadential figure in the bass and the wavering of the syncopated chords, until the development begins.

We have described the principal features of the music rather as facts of structure than in their larger aspect as vehicles of expression. But if they are also observed as portraying states of mental tension and motor impulse, the infinite hesitant kindliness with which the music lays its hand upon us can hardly fail to be realized. The composer commands us to play *mit der innigsten Empfindung*; he would perhaps have resented our very general words as an attempt to give sharpened definition to his direction; but it will be evident that only the minutest observation of all that is implied in his notes can guide the fingers to any true revelation of their meaning.

The following movement fulfills the function of the scherzo in the four-movement scheme of this sonata. (The first movement, having an exposition, a development, and a recapitulation, bears considerable resemblance to the conventional "sonata form"; but it lacks the first essential of that form — a co-ordinate, justly contrasted second subject. The last movement, however, amply fills out that design.) We have no space for detailed examination of this second movement; yet, since we shall study very minutely the following brief *Adagio*, some hint of the manner in which that movement is approached is necessary.

It is no such simple outburst of gaiety as satisfied Beethoven in his earlier adventures in this form. Under an animated and apparently capricious surface he has managed to cloak what turns out to be another aspect of the same profound gentleness. Such blitheness of motion as is here pictured is far beyond the limbs of man to execute; but it is not beyond his imagination to trip thus lightly upon whatever surface will give support to the limbs of fancy, and it was only in this region that Beethoven could give rein to that gayer tone which the gentleness already pictured might assume. Analysis of the music would in some measure substantiate this opinion; but we must turn to a still more difficult task.

The ensuing *Adagio* is surely one of the most poetic utterances in all literature. The nature of our task will compel us to attempt some phrases descriptive of its character, but we shall delay these until the music has been examined minutely in the light of its elemental and accessory expressive values. We studied the Brünnhilde theme in similarly minute detail, with explanatory comment at each step; but a more concise and schematic statement should now be intelligible. We shall study only the first eight bars (Ex. 23) and shall present our findings phrase by phrase:

Ex. 23

Phrase I (Bars 1–2)

Motion

(a) slow (*Adagio*); 4-8 time rather than 2-4.

(b) elastic: propulsive, active harmony on "one," coming to rest on "three," but with residue of momentum sufficient for melodic rise to C and the ensuing dip to G♯.

(c) similar activity of both melody and harmony on "one" of bar 2.

(d) cadence masculine, but on "three," and so unemphatic.

Tension

(a) artificial activity of initial note (dominant seventh harmony, first and second inversions).

(b) melodic rise (E to C) on rest tones (see b, above) with tension of position only.

(c) most active note (G♯) on "one" of bar 2; activity increased by descent of diminished 4th and by dominant seventh harmony, second and third inversions.

(d) similar bass design in both bars emphasizes the more active inversions of the harmony.

(e) phrase-end on first inversion of tonic chord with a "settling" figure of 32nds in melody (see d, above).

Accessory Values

(a) low register, *una corda*, making perceptible the very slightest dynamic gradations.

(b) clinging agogic stress on "down-beats."

(c) extreme legato throughout.

(d) rhetorical emphasis coincides with rhythmic, on G♯.

(e) the whole phrase, being "antecedent," tentative in utterance.

Phrase II (Bars 3–4)

Motion

(a) more active than in I — shorter notes, more frequent harmonic change; opening motive (8th-note, E | 8th, E, over the bar-line) becomes, twice within bar 3, two 16ths + 8th, and in bar 4, two 16ths + two 16ths + 8th, giving feminine cadence.

(b) up-beat (bar 2) gives rhythmic propulsion; this, continued on all strong beats and intensified by active harmony, accounts for rise to F and the more expanded curve of bar 4.

Tension

(a) reiteration of E with concordant, then discordant harmony coinciding with down-beat emphasis.

(b) resolutions of discordant or active harmony unstable and brief.

(c) disjunct approach to B♭ gives sense of weakened resistance.

(d) intense discord (VI₇) on first down-beat; discord thereafter progressively softer and darker, with influence of Neapolitan 6th conspicuous.

(e) feminine cadence lengthened and made portentous by harmonic fading from major to minor (G♯–G♮).

Accessory Values

(a) rhetorical stresses on F (bar 3) and E (bar 4) enhance tensions and fading noted in (d) and (e) above.

(b) bar 3 slightly more intense than bar 4; new color for Neapolitan 6th, with slight agogic emphasis of G♮ at end of cadence to prepare next phrase.

(c) maintain prescribed *una corda*; extreme legato.

Phrase III (Bars 5–6)

Motion

(a) even steps (no divided beats) with high F lengthened to suggest poise of attainment and give point to long drop beginning Phrase IV.

(b) ascent in long but effortless strides, each new upward step begun on pitch-level attained by preceding step.

(c) each new level attained on discord, giving propulsion for next stride.

(d) masculine ending, on V₇ of C major, expectant as in (a) above.

Tension

(a) alternate concord and discord (note c, above); but initial e-minor triad (because of lowering of G♯ to G♮ preceding) obscure in tonality and so somewhat active.

(b) conjunct downward bass increases apparent altitude of melodic ascent.

(c) close on V₇ gives tension accordant with motion noted in (d) above.

Accessory Values

(a) careful variation of dynamics, always in *pp, una corda*, to mark rhythmic weights of repeated melodic notes (see b, under Motion); barely perceptible *dim.* at end to mark "vanishing-point."

(b) slight retardation in bar 6, with minute agogic delay of final chord.

Phrase IV (Bars 7–8)

Motion

(a) still in deliberate pattern of III, slightly activated by 16th-note upbeat and by even, then dotted, 16ths, to reach quiet feminine cadence.

(b) conjunct, contrasting with disjunct in III; leap to G prepared by rise on B–C♯–D; rise thereafter gives a singular sense of attainment.

Tension

(a) whole bar quietly dissonant; rhetorical stress on D "rhymes" with that on preceding high F.

(b) delayed (but assured) establishment of tonic harmony in expanded feminine cadence.

(c) tension of position (rising) contributes to attainment noted in (b) above.

Accessory Values

(a) richer, thicker tone in low register fully realized (always *pp*, *una corda*).

(b) chief rhetorical emphasis on D (bar 7); that on G (bar 8) secondary, since cadence is imminent.

(c) diminution with slight agogic expansion to the assured cadence (see b, above).

More repellent presentation of the molecular substance suggestive of profound idea could hardly be devised than that which has just been offered. The mere additive sum of the items listed will not yield even a coherent verbal notion of the music, to say nothing of the profundity we have claimed for it. But these items have not been presented as the pieces of a verbal jig-saw puzzle, requiring only the patience of indolent curiosity to fit them into a design equivalent to the musical idea. Each item describes a characteristic feature — or some characteristic of a feature — of that idea; each, apprehended accordingly as an attribute of the music, seems to illuminate that idea; and in this light the music itself emerges as vastly more communicative of experience than its design, contemplated as mere design, could ever be.

The items have in fact been presented, through their classification into categories as elements and accessories of expression, as objectively as possible. As items of structure they will probably be acceptable without dissent. But in their aspect as factors in the process of expression, where these facts of structure fuse, that fusion may be differently observed and interpreted by different hearers. We can offer, therefore, no more than our own interpretation of this fusion, together with some of the contributions to the more than musical idea which associative increment adds to the communication offered by the elements themselves.

Like the word "strange" in our illustrative poetic stanza, the first chord in the *Adagio* gains in meaning through antithesis with something gone before. For the previous movement closes in F major, and this E major chord, as it strikes our ear, may have many meanings, but it means nothing in the key of F. Our imaginative sensibility, plunged thus into momentary tonal obscurity, is aroused. Low register and the slow but intrinsically active motion, embodied in rich, softly sonorous tone, add to our expectancy of imaginative adventure. Propelled by the initial harmonic unrest, the long E, attaining concord (on "three") reveals its momentum in a preliminary turn and an easy upward leap. In the dissonance there is no harshness, yet its gentle propulsion is irresistible; and in the upward leap, from the attained concord, there is neither effort nor the excitement of action, but only a high awareness of spiritual quietude.

But this quietude is itself a kind of ecstasy; and as we realize it we discover that the melodic line which portrayed it is largely similar in pattern to that which depicted the ecstasy of Brünnhilde. Differences in motion, tension, and atmosphere are apparent in every note: rest where there was activity; changing, where there was persistent harmony; rhetorical stress not at the peak of the melodic curve but on the dip thereafter, imparting to the ensuing cadence ("imperfect" because the tonic chord is inverted) both quietude and unfulfilled implication.

This is no love music. Here is no breathless expectancy, no anticipatory, passionate warmth, no self-centered delight. Rather, there is the understanding bred of fruitful retrospection — an extraverted gentleness profound even to ecstasy.

With this note of feeling established, the next phrase — more poignant in dissonance — becomes, without the hint of bitterness which in another context it might convey, only the deeper in sympathy. The third phrase ascends on upborne harmonies to a region where celestial things are glimpsed; and the last, with its extraordinary change of register, seems to put the seal of truth upon the revelation just seen.

We have not quoted, and shall not analyze, beyond this point. You will find the opening motive, in the bass, quietly answered in higher octaves. Then it is hastened (by "diminution") into a form similar in contour to the *Liebestod* motive — here utterly shorn of worldly passion, but glowing with a warmth which cannot but be colored by our remembrance of its origin. An indeterminate (and most appropriate) end on an unresolved dominant chord brings, after a moment of improvisatory contemplation, an exquisite reminiscence of the first movement of the sonata — a confirmation, surely, of the relation in expressive sense (for there is no re-semblance in structure) which our comment will have suggested between the two movements.

This reminiscence serves also as an approach to the Finale — a move-ment quite regularly in sonata form, whose development is a long fugue on a theme expanded out of the opening motive of the first subject. The tone of the whole piece is indicated in Beethoven's superscription, *Gesch-wind, doch nicht zu sehr, und mit Entschlossenheit* (Fast, but not too much so, and with determination). Immediate relativity to the implications we have found in the earlier movements might be tentatively suggested if we were to fall into the error, already noted, of taking successive musical "events" in a narrative sense. The antithesis of feeling is so high that a direct relation in character — in spite of the reminiscent introduction — is not apparent; yet there is somehow a high appropriateness in the frank energy of the music. In the second subject however, beginning at bar 33, there is a lilting joyousness * which seems the perfect complement, not only of the opening decisiveness, but of the whole sense of the sonata.†

Greater heights of interest than are reached in this music have hardly been attained. The coming romantic attitude is here clearly foreshadowed — in substance but not in that often unfortunate manner whose colorful surfaces hid, even from its practitioners, so much of fascinating untruth.

It is no secret that untruth can be uttered with convincing vehemence. The elements of expression are vehicles for utterance; but like language

* Schnabel, in his edition of the sonatas, offers as a guide to the sense of this theme the inexplicable suggestion *non lirico*. How the hesitant, elastic, off-beat repetitions of the first note A, and the swerving leaps of the succeeding phrases as well, can be seen as other than lyrical in the highest degree passes our comprehen-sion.

† It should be confessed that not all the meaning we have read out of the music we have analyzed was derived from those phrases alone. The sonata is dedicated to Beethoven's former pupil, Dorothea Ertmann. Her husband, an officer in the Austrian army, was stationed in Italy. While they were there, Dorothea's only re-maining child, a little boy, died. Dorothea's grief was so great that her mind was endangered, and the general, hoping for relief, managed to be transferred back to Vienna.

Dorothea did not improve. But one day she went, unheralded, to visit Beethoven, who knew of her condition. His greeting to her was something like this: "I think we shall speak together in music this afternoon"; and he began to improvise for her. Dorothea wept and was comforted.

Whether this music or any single phrase of it is preserved from that improvisa-tion is unknown. The incident itself is a fact. But it seems to us that the utterances we have examined — of course, not directly consolatory in tone — voice such gen-tleness and wisdom as might lift the cloud of bereavement from a mind all but dis-traught.

they offer, as vehicles, no criterion of the truthfulness of what they utter. That criterion lies in the discriminations bred in the world of experience. Our elements exist through their relation to experience; but, like words, they are equally at the disposal of the liar and the seeker for truth. But the musical liar, like the demagogic orator, will be caught out in the end by him who applies the criterion of experience in his criticism of music.

For experience is felt as well as known. We demand the evidence of feeling as well as of fact. Indeed, feeling appears, for whoever lives in the world of experience, as the seal of truth set upon that which is factually understood in experience; and he who falsifies feeling is a more dangerous liar than he who falsifies fact.

Almost all the music we have examined appears true. But a brief study is in order of the manner in which the elements of expression may be used for the utterance of false feeling.

Feeling may prove false in two ways. It may itself be so cleverly trumped up as to appear genuine (the *Sehnsucht nach Sehnsucht* of the weaker romanticists); or it may be the genuine reaction to a misinterpreted (and to that extent a trumped-up) experience. In either case, genuineness or falsity is impossible to determine without insight into the experience which has generated the feeling. This insight, at best, has seldom the certainty of a scientific conclusion. But where, as with music, the generative experience is not portrayed but must be inferred from the feeling actually expressed, the discrimination of falsity — although essential to understanding — is precarious.

Yet we have constantly to make such discriminations — drawn by inference from evidence of emotion aroused by unrevealed fact — in everyday life. *Savoir-faire* is the product of precisely such an intuitive skill. And if art is to be viewed as an illumination of life, a counterpart of that same skill which we exercise every day must be reckoned as somehow operable in the field of art.

Even in the field of representative art, where the life to be illuminated is to a certain degree factually portrayed, these discriminations are uncertain — as witness the divergent "interpretations" of *Hamlet*. In the field of music, where direct reference to objective facts of experience is all but impossible, the burden placed on the intuition is heavier — so heavy that the studious music lover may indeed feel that the only factual object offered to the intuition is structure, and that the feeling it expresses can be only the feeling for form.

But what is this image of structure — this image whose valuation yields his idea of form? Candidly observed, his image proves to have been to a great extent concocted. Its underlying propositions have indeed been drawn from the music of great composers. Yet they have been drawn therefrom, not by the composers themselves but by theorists; the vision of the theorists must have been colored by their particular judgments of value; and their propositions may thus prove to have been drawn from great music only in order to exalt that vision of greatness which instigated their theoretical search.

In any case they are manifestations of structural rather than of creative principles, *and to the extent to which they pretend to expound the creative act*, they are trumped-up principles; the "purely" musical experience they define is a trumped-up experience; and the feeling aroused by musical art as comprising no more than structure is — *to the extent to which it fails to reflect and illuminate experience beyond that of structure* — false feeling.

Our italics emphasize a qualification of high import. We have not denied that the feeling engendered by a consummate achievement in structure is real. But if we re-define the word structure so as to make it embrace the whole essentially communicative substance of the art-work, we embark on a dangerous adventure in semantics. For, to the extent to which form fuses with meaning, more than that fact of high organization which the word structure denotes may be resident in form. Indeed, in so far as form is seen as appropriate to meaning,* this fusion *must* occur; and the intuitive perception which we are calling expression is fed by this more than pure structure. The surface of this more than pure structure can indeed be analyzed, and its apparent purport expounded, in terms descriptive of structure only; but to do this is to practice a deception which fatally distorts the true purpose of art. For while structure arises from the altogether genuine experience of organization, art arises from a vastly larger area of experience.

In our analyses thus far we have largely avoided this question of genuineness or falsity in feeling. It was implied in our discussion of the F major Mozart sonata, and was distinctly visible in our comparison of the two funeral marches. In one of those, the vision of experience was vast; in the

---

* Consider the confusion resulting from an inversion of this proposition — "in so far as meaning is seen as appropriate to form." The notion is all but inconceivable. Yet this notion, veiled in verbiage, is the notion of "pure" art.

other, restricted. In both, the experience confronted was genuine. So, doubtless, was the feeling, which in each case corresponded to the vision. But Chopin's restricted vision evoked an over-emphasis — made the more obvious by the comparison — which we there described as self-excited, but which in our present perspective may be labeled as false. This will serve to illustrate the second of the two types of false feeling (that resulting from misinterpreted experience) noted above.

It is also possible to portray in music feeling which resembles the reaction to genuine experience, but which proves upon examination to be an adventure in feeling merely, lacking any sound basis in actual experience.* Such adventures are all too common, whether in life or in music.

The Liszt Sonata in B minor appears, in our present perspective, to be such an adventure. In the more usual perspective, it will be seen as a rather interesting adventure in the mechanics of structure. Ernest Hutcheson, in *The Literature of the Piano* (Knopf, 1948), describes it so. For in this work, as in his symphonic poems and symphonies, Liszt employed extensively the musical device of thematic transformation. This device was not really new. It had been largely developed by fifteenth-century masters and by later polyphonists. But in that rapid evolution of the program-idea which was presently to generate the Wagnerian leading-motive, themes and their transformations were made to take on a definiteness of meaning far sharper than they could have had in earlier periods.†

If we examine critically the opening of this sonata, what does its elemental substance convey of actual emotional utterance? There is first a

* There can of course be no question as to the truth or falsity of feeling when it is observed, psychologically, simply as a phenomenon of nervous excitement. That question arises only when feeling is observed in relation to its cause.

† It is impossible to determine just when and in what degree of vividness themes and their alterations began to take on the objective significance we have learned to attach to the leading-motive. The basic theme of Bach's *Art of Fugue* undergoes a bewildering variety of alterations into which it would be easy — and of course quite gratuitous — to read the sense of leading-motives. But Albert Schweitzer had no scruple against defining certain general types of pattern as motives (e.g., the descending chromatic scale as a motive of grief, in the *Crucifixus* of the B-minor Mass, the F-minor Three-part Invention, and elsewhere). Mozart's three introductory chords in the Overture to *The Magic Flute* are generally interpreted as having significance referable to Masonic ritual. Beethoven, in the *Egmont* Overture uses the saraband rhythm (supposedly Spanish) to suggest the sinister influence of Alva and the Spanish Inquisition, and he transforms this phrase together with its pleading pendant into the second subject of the ensuing *Allegro*. And Berlioz, in his *Fantastic Symphony*, used his theme for the *idée fixe* with a variety of suggestion hardly distinguishable from that offered by many a Wagnerian motive.

hesitant, tonally obscure suggestion of gloom, conveyed by a somewhat distorted minor scale which, after its off-beat beginning on what prove to be pedal G's, descends with rhythmic decision. The suggestion is left indeterminate, but is strong enough to arouse expectancy. Then the *Lento assai* tempo is abandoned and leaping G's initiate the first subject group with the theme illustrated in the accompanying example (Ex. 24).

Ex. 24

It has a staggering sort of motion, indicative of such extreme perturbation as would be exhibited only by an actor in the most lurid melodrama; and its tone-stresses — or rather, its one tone-stress, that of the diminished seventh — appearing in the context of the introduction, seems to display no more than the surface of distress. One cannot but suspect this to be the surface of a trumped-up experience.

There ensues at once a complementary theme (Ex. 25) whose immediate expressive suggestion appears as a kind of anxiety, conveyed by the rapidly repeated notes, by the relatively meaningless upward leap of a fifth (being no more than a continuation of the already established B-minor tonality, it adds nothing to the tone-stress), and by its indeterminate ending on a chromatic descent to the unstable sub-dominant harmony, and then to the still vaguer but already characteristic diminished seventh. This

Ex. 25

character is in some measure imparted by the context of the preceding thought. Observed in isolation, or in another context, it might show various shades of rather sinister energy; in a high register, it might appear humorous or sardonic; but in its present association it does little more than sharpen the focus of our attention on the futile agitation of the preceding theme.

But what are we to make of this theme when, through the simple device of augmentation and the support of a liquid harmonization in the major key, it is turned (as in Ex. 26) into a languishing phrase of love? And how shall we relate to its original sense the opening theme (Ex. 24)

Ex. 26

which, by an obvious rhythmic transformation akin to diminution, is made to sing another verse of the same song?

Ex. 27

No attentive listener would fail to note the similarity of these transformations to their originals. But while the structural relation is obvious, the expressive relation is disconcerting. It becomes a Jekyll-Hyde affair, no more credible than Stevenson's miracle, but lacking the point which, in the story, justifies the miracle.

The reader will doubtless detect, at this point, an apparent flaw in our argument relative to the persistence of meaning in varied examples of a single type of tone-stress or motion. For we formerly insisted that the pattern of the Brünnhilde theme retained some of its ecstatic quality even when it appeared in different compositions and in different guises. Now we are insisting that the transformations of two themes, within the same composition, show little or no expressive relevancy to their originals.

The contradiction, however, is not as complete as it seems. Thematic transformation (as here, and also in more formal sets of variations) must retain enough resemblance to the original pattern to be recognizable as a *structural* variant. But expressiveness is not the product of any and every structural note-sequence.* It is a product of those note-sequences which, while of course structurally patterned, display the particular character-

---

* Deryck Cooke (*op. cit.*; see our Appendix, p. 191) assigns all but verbally precise feeling-character to his "tonal tensions" — an error (as we see it) disastrous to any real subtlety of expression.

istics of motion and tension which represent the tensions and motor impulses of feeling. But that act of perception which recognizes structural pattern is not the same act of perception as that which recognizes feeling-character. Retention or alteration of expressive relations of motion or tension will indeed imply retained or altered expressive sense; but the persistence of note-pattern, merely as tone-sequence but with its characteristics of motion and tension transformed, is no guarantee that the expressive meaning resident in the original version of a theme will be retained in that mere pattern.

The Liszt sonata, then, although it displays much structural ingenuity in the transformation of its themes, and although it yields — the transformations once effected — sections of coherent and by no means unmoving musical discourse in the character of that transformation, is a composition whose experiential basis is essentially fantastic, and whose whole conveyance of meaning is similarly unrelated to genuine experience. It appears, after critical dissection in the search for a possible truth of expression, merely an ingenious exercise in structural variation, episodic and irrelevant.

X

The Contribution of the Elements to the Problem of Criticism

W E MIGHT have gone on, endlessly, analyzing and comparing in the aspect of their expressive significance works both earlier and later than our chosen examples; but these, we believe, will sufficiently illustrate our thesis— that music is capable of expressing, intelligibly, emotions aroused by significant human experience. The present chapter will attempt both to show the nature of the problem of musical criticism when the expressiveness of music is recognized as a factor in it, and also (but with little resort to the apparatus of analysis) how an expanded critical view of the significance of musical compositions results from consideration of their reference to knowable human experience. A succinct statement of the problem may precede our illustrations.

Criticism is literally judgment — a judgment of values. Value, in an object to be criticized, is assessed by observing that object in those lights which reveal not only the substance and the organization of the object, but also its purpose. Although purpose may be so obvious as to be ignored, it is still one of the ultimate criteria of value; for a purposeless object is fit only for the waste-basket. This formula for criticism is clearly valid for objects of utility. It is also valid for works of art.

Any art-work is composed of a substance, in itself in variable degree sensuously appealing, which is organized in a manner also appellant to our more intellectual apprehension of order. This organization yields what is superficially recognized as the form of the work. The percept of form, however, embraces both the sensuous appeal of the substance and the organization of the work, as well as a possible aspect of its purpose.

Since substance and organization appear, and normally are contemplated, simultaneously, there appears at the very outset of critical appraisal a fusion of impressions which complicates the problem of criticism. For a fusion of compatible values yields a product which will be rated higher than the sum of those individual values observed in isolation. A merely utilitarian object — for example, a Revere sauce-pan with a copper bottom applied to its stainless steel substance — presents this fusion of substance and design, together with a taken-for-granted intimation of its purpose.

But by comparison with such a merely utilitarian object, a work of art, even when observed only for its substance and its organization, will be ranked very high. For not only is its uncommon substance more carefully selected and refined. Organization enhances far more highly the intrinsic interest of the substance. Form, thus attained, is in itself a purpose achieved — a purpose hardly to be compared with that of the utilitarian sauce-pan, and yet a purpose not foreign to the desires and the needs of a sentient mind.

Neither those needs nor their satisfaction is of the utilitarian order. Thus the artist who, concerned with substance and organization alone, achieves a perfect form may properly be called an abstractionist. For his form, as we have already noted, has been achieved through a drawing away (an abstraction) *from* the world of concrete and utilitarian things and experiences, and the satisfactions he offers are those belonging to the similarly abstracted "world" of art.

No one will call this world undesirable or even unreal. For the satisfactions it offers are derived from the not unfamiliar substance of his art (tone, word, marble, color, or whatever), and attained through processes of organization by no means unknown in the larger world of experience. But by comparison with this grosser world, the world of abstract art must be acknowledged to be both narrow and hard to enter. Only through relevancy to experience regarded as significant in this larger world can the artist's work there win approval.

His problem will thus indeed be enlarged. He must adjust the handling of his cherished substance, not merely toward the realization of an ideal of perfect form, but also toward the reflection — through that ideal form — of the desires and needs generated by non-artistic experience. Since to be art at all his work must have an ideal form, it will still be an abstraction. But this time it will be achieved by drawing its essence *out of* the world of experience, rather than by drawing *away from* that world.

The vast preponderance of extant art is of this order. Its method, until quite recently, has been to interpret experience through the frank representation of indicative facts of experience — even (as we are contending in the case of music) the emotions born of experience, which are also indicative facts. Art of this order is nowadays described as "representative," suggesting a fundamental antithesis to "abstract" art.

This antithesis almost invariably proves to be an exaggeration. Even that art which professes to "contain" no other than the values of substance and form is not wholly abstracted away from the concrete experience the abstract artist shuns. For there is no "purely" artistic substance; neither is any artistic organization wholly unrelated to familiar experience of organization. The words "abstract" and "representative," therefore, do not designate *categories* of art. They designate no more than divergent artistic *methods*; and art, however dependent on method for its existence, is not itself method, nor can its full value be critically assessed in terms of method. Its value lies in the idea it evokes in the observer; and if that remains, for the observer, an idea of method or process or structure only, then either the artist or the observer is at fault.

We have defined an idea as an image and a valuation of experience. However precarious that definition, it seems to us that the essential idea of any art-work, and also the more highly abstract notion of art itself, may be subsumed thereunder. Art, in our view, must somehow project or evoke an image of experience and — if it is to appeal to dwellers outside the realm of "pure" art — of experience wider than that of organization merely, although the fact of organization will contribute incalculably to the vividness of the image.

To be commonly understood, the imaged experience must be rooted in what may be called, in the largest sense, known facts of experience. That is to say, the artist does not create for himself alone, but to communicate his vision of experience to the observer of his work.* Neither for the artist nor for his observer is this experience a mere accumulation of correlated facts. Correlation is indeed the product of a higher mental activity

* Cf. Wagner, in *Oper und Drama*, Part II, Sec. II: Der Mensch ist auf zwiefache Weise Dichter: in der *Anschauung* und in der *Mittheilung*. Die *natürliche* Dichtungsgabe ist die Fähigkeit, die seinen Sinnen von Aussen sich kundgebenden Erscheinungen zu einem inneren Bilde von ihnen sich zu verdichten; die *künstleriche*, dieses Bild nach Aussen wieder mitzutheilen. (Man is Poet in a two-fold sense: through *perception* and through *communication*. The *natural* poetic gift is the ability to create, from the appearances impinging on his senses from [the world] without [i.e., through perception] an inner image of their nature; the *artistic*, the ability to communicate this image again [to the world] without.)

155

than mere perception. But the mind which perceives and correlates facts is also *self*-conscious; in any awareness of correlated fact this consciousness of self will be mingled; and that mind's store of accumulated and correlated fact — its experience — will then be interpreted by that same mind according to its immediate or future interest.

Such interpretation cannot but be an act of imagination. A single encountered incident, whether physical or portrayed, will be perceived differently by all who encounter it. It will also be differently valued, not only against the background of each individual's factual experience but in the light of his immediate interest. For this interest, while in part a product and a reflection of the individual's factual experience, is also *self*-interest. Self-interest, involving the well-being of the self, is to that extent emotional. Contemplating future as well as immediate consequences, it is also imaginative.

There is high similarity, however, in the reactions of similarly experienced minds, whether to real or to virtual experience. If this were not so, there would be no society. There would also be no art. For art is a portrayal of the essence of experience — of life as it is felt, not only by the artist but by the society of which he is a part. If the observer of art (also a part of that society) had no imagination, the artist's effort would be useless. But the observer, contemplating the artist's portrayal of experience, may share in his imaginative effort and become, at least at the moment of comprehension, himself perceptively (as Wagner held) an artist. But the bond between him and the artist is not in the field of artistic skill. What unites them is the bond of common experience.

Yet the artist, interpreting experience in terms of his special skill, is also working in a field of experience — one which his observer can hardly share. The boundary between that special field and the larger area of experience (quite possibly more familiar to the observer than to the artist) is not sharply marked. The artist's creative attention — of necessity sharply focussed on problems of structure — may recede unconsciously from the larger into this narrower field of experience. The observer, more readily than the artist, will note this recession which, for him, will appear as a departure from the familiar and fertile field of experience into the unfamiliar and barren area of technique. Artist and observer may each, of course, enlarge his understanding of the other's field. But they who possess only the imaginative powers of the observer must continue to form most of the artist's public; and so long as this is true the final judgment of artistic effort will be rendered — whether through conscious analysis or by intuitive preference — in favor of that which intelligibly interprets the essence of experience as society encounters it.

Music claims sisterhood with the other arts. It could hardly maintain this claim if it had no commerce with the general field of experience. Even the vague notion of music as a universal language is a heedless but indicative recognition of the soundness of the claim. But if that claim can be defended not only upon the vague recognition but upon some tangible definition of the relation of music to experience, then such definition as our elements of expression seem to offer may prove a valuable addition to the apparatus of criticism.

It may also contribute, more obviously, to the re-creative process of performance — to the "interpretation" of compositions which, in our definition at least, are themselves interpretations of experience. Something akin to that skill which we noted a moment ago as likely to disturb the composer's focus upon the originative field of experience operates, more conspicuously, in that shaping into actual tone by which the performer transforms written musical symbols into audible communications of musical idea.

We described those devices for effective musical utterance which in large part comprise the performer's technique — his apparatus of communication — as accessory values of musical expression. For unless there existed a prior fact of musical composition to which they were appropriate (the composer's apparatus of communication), these devices would be mere exercises in inflection: purposeless and fit only for the wastebasket.

We have seen that the technique of composition may itself be similarly misused. Our criterion for the detection of such misuse was that of the relativity of the composition to experience. We see no reason to abandon that criterion. To employ it, however, necessitates a sharper definition of the word experience than that word usually connotes. For we must think of experience as that whole store of awareness, implanted in the memory through the contact of the self with the external world, which is available through association for comparisons and judgments of value when new objects or conditions, whether in the world or in the self, are encountered.

Relativity is patently the basis of such associative selection. But relativity, thus incessantly sought in the assessment of values in new objects, may itself become an "object" — a fact of organization, abstracted out of the more obvious association between concrete objects, but no less real than they to the "experienced" mind.

The idea of Form, thus abstracted *out of* perceived realities of organization, is thus still an image and a valuation of experience. It may be, for him who also chooses to abstract his self *from* the ordinary world of experience, the highest of attainable ideal values. It is not so for the world at large, where preoccupation with ephemeral encounters yields pitiably narrow valuations of really significant experience. But there are also, in this larger world, percipient minds capable of abstracting out of the the general experience of the world and of the self, the meaning of this experience. For them the idea of Form, when abstracted out of the larger world, is richer in substance — and perhaps not less truly ideal — than that of the purist. And for them the valuation of art demands to be established upon that same basis which yields their valuation of life. Art objectifies for them the essence of mature and pondered experience; and music, if it aspires to sisterhood with the other arts, must be similarly evaluated.

Composers, for whom the stuff of music — more obviously than for the world at large — is a kind of symbol for the essence of experience, have often testified to their expressive purpose.* Their interpreters — the performers — schooled by teachers no more percipient than themselves, and preoccupied with the abundant problems offered by what we have called the accessory values of expression, substitute technical proficiency and musical intuition largely guided by that proficiency, for what, in our view, might be a keener insight into the composer's expressive purpose.

Yet that purpose, in the most authentic critical literature we possess

* Compare, for example, the comment of Dr. Quickelberg, to whom Lasso's *Penitential Psalms* expressed so vividly the sense of the words that it was "as if you saw the experience before your very eyes." Or that of Handel who, praised for the great pleasure his *Messiah* had given the audience, responded: "Pleasure? I hoped to make them better." Or of Beethoven who, as we have already noted, is credibly reported as saying that if the world really understood the import of his music there would be no more war.

This last remark, in the view of practical politicians, will doubtless appear as the most unreal of idealistic visions. But should their cautious efforts toward the same end ever succeed (of which outcome those very practical men have no hope) Beethoven's musical utterances may come to appear as a vastly more competent forecast of the spiritual conditions essential to that end than were all the machinations and dickerings of the diplomats.

(that provided by the musicologists) is all but ignored. Exhaustive investigation of both instrumental structure and the techniques of performance in the music of by-gone days (*Auffuhrüngspraxis*) has determined with indisputable exactness many characteristics of tone production and tone combination as they must have existed in (for example) Bach's time.* The leading of the voices (instrumental or vocal) in Bach's intricate polyphony comes out, as a result, with most gratifying clarity. In so far as the design of music comprises the meaning of music, performance according to these prescriptions enormously clarifies its meaning. But in so far as that music has meaning external to that of design, musicology as a science is silent. How far the performances of that day revealed that meaning, and how far its revelation was demanded by its hearers, we have only the occasional over-enthusiastic comments of observers to inform us. But we do have the texture of Bach's scores — a texture not only impeccable in every structural aspect, but one in which the elements of musical expression as we have described them seem to reveal the primary creative purpose. Such a purpose appeared in our study of the C♯-minor Fugue. Much briefer examination of other examples will show that it operated, decisively, in determining the original and the final concept of the work. We shall look at a few numbers from the great Mass in B minor.

The opening *Kyrie* — a prodigious Fugue — is prefaced by a kind of Prelude, only four bars long, and thematically quite independent of the Fugue, but anticipating with the highest intensity the religious attitude which underlies not only the Fugue but all the rest of the Mass. Such intensity would be unthinkable if the two words were taken in the context of the Roman Catholic ritual. In the individualistic Lutheran view, their boldness, if startling, is wholly appropriate. But it is clear, at once, that a whole theology existed as the background of experience out of which this music originated.

The Fugue itself is of unexampled weight and majesty. These qualities are patent to any ear. (Even musicology sometimes allows itself the use of such suggestive terms.) But the creative image embraced more than is suggested by these really adjectival terms. The music is addressed to the First Person of the Trinity; and to the portrayal of that substantive image

---

* Not only harpsichords and clavichords and organs, but many wind instruments, now obsolete, have been reconstructed; the constitution of early orchestras and choirs has been determined; and even the art of ornamentation — a skill so far left to the performer that only compact symbols, extremely variable in meaning, indicated the nature of the ornament — has been largely systematized.

(for Bach real, not virtual) the hearer should perceive that his boundless imaginative energy was devoted.

The *Christe eleison*, although obviously more stylized, still reveals that tenderness with which Bach looks upon the Son. And the following *Kyrie eleison*, with its hushed and mysterious theme, its diminished 3rd clinging obscurely to the F♯ it embraces, is just as certainly addressed to the Third Person of the Trinity. The six words of text for these three pieces do indeed imply for the believer a whole theology. Bach's music, in the character of his themes and in every detail of their elaboration, shows that for him this theology has become a philosophy.

Is it enough to perform these pieces (the instruments are as eloquent as the voices) merely as the extraordinary examples of polyphony which they certainly are? Was it Bach's whole purpose to engage the purely musical interest of his listeners?

The rest of the Mass, of course in varying degree, shows the same imaginative depth. The jubilant *Gloria* is frank enough to shock the sanctimonious, but is a wonderful reflection of that literalness of imagery which imbues all Bach's theology. The ensuing *Et in terra pax*, ornamented with Baroque floridity, is still for the penetrating reader, as fervent a prayer for peace as any ever uttered. (He sees, more clearly than Beethoven, that if inward peace is attained, there will be no need to pray for outward peace.) The sheer beauty of the Latin text, *Qui tollis peccata mundi*, is mirrored in the wonderful texture of the music (the orchestral accompaniment, without the voices, is a complete piece in itself); but the sense of that text is still more vividly projected.

The *Credo* begins with an astounding contrapuntal manipulation of the age-old Gregorian strain to which *Credo in unum Deum* had been sung. But that strain, in its elemental stress (particularly in the upward inflection for *Deum*) is itself singularly appropriate to the attitude of mind in which it is sung, and Bach's rhythmic broadening only amplifies its sense. And the incessant recurrence of the theme, often at aurally unexpected intervals, seems to reflect the implied unanimity, not only of the present congregation but of all Christendom, in the utterance of the words. The drop of a major 7th for the last syllable of *Patrem omnipotentem* is an imaginative feat of high vividness. *Et in unum Deum*, somewhat drily doctrinal in its canonic symbolism, softens marvelously as it approaches (with *qui propter nos*, etc.) the central mystery of the Incarnation; and that scene, painted in shifting harmonies rather than in definite melodic lines, is all bathed in orchestral starlight. The *Crucifixus* (on a four-bar passacaglia-bass, 13 times repeated, but never, except by pedants, particularly noticed in performance) seems, in historic perspective, the most vivid and novel adventure in expressive harmony in all the literature of music.

We must resist the temptation to pursue further our cursory study of the Mass. It must be evident that the text itself either states or implies, for the believer, facts contributory to religious experience. In themselves, these facts do not immediately suggest music. Interpreted, however, they are of high import — of import so high that it is beyond purely intellectual conception. They yield an image of experience involving both the facts themselves and the self of the believer.

It is evident, not only in the extraordinary outcry with which the Mass opens but throughout its whole substance, that Bach's was a Lutheran self. It is also evident that his mind, as it conceived this valuation of the Lutheran image of religious experience, was focussed on that image. To the "realization" of it in terms of tone, he devoted all his technical skill. To observe that skill is to be amazed — but not in the way Bach intended that we should be amazed. Of course, being an artist, he exercised his technical powers to the utmost; of course, his artistry is visible to those who understand artistry; but like the contrivers of the text he set (who were themselves no inconsiderable artists) he was primarily concerned with the experience he was portraying, and his artistry was guided by that concern whether in the invention or in the manipulation of his representative artistic substance. Without that guidance — in itself not intrinsically musical — we should have had from him something quite other than this masterpiece of masterpieces.

The believer in absolute music may still object that (as with our first illustrative example) verbal knowledge of the experience offers the basis and the substance of that meaning which we have found resident in the music — that we have read that meaning into the music out of the text. The two do indeed offer, in general, similar images and similar valuations of the religious experience. But the current of meaning does not always flow from words into music. It may also flow from music into words — and may find that outlet long after the musical idea has been fully expressed. A striking instance may be adduced.

While Bach was at Cöthen, little occupied with religious music, he composed many great instrumental works. Among these was a huge concerto in D minor for violin. The original of that work is lost; but he fortunately transcribed it for harpsichord, and that version we possess. The first movement is of a towering energy, maintained and amplified incredibly. The second, based on a somewhat freely treated passacaglia-bass, is a miracle of somber profundity. Many years later, at Leipzig where he was engaged with the five complete cycles of church cantatas he is said to have written, he took as text for one of these the passage from Acts, XIV, 22: *Wir müssen durch viel Trübsal in das Reich Gottes eingehen* (We must through much tribulation enter the kingdom of heaven). For prologue, he rearranged the first movement, making over the solo part for organ. For the opening chorus, set to the text just quoted, he took the slow movement of the concerto, almost verbatim (including the solo melody that was originally for violin), and to this already rich and satisfying texture he added four florid choral voices, musically quite effortless, and yet spiritually absorbed with the sense of the text. (Emphasis is made to fall successively on *wir*, on *müssen*, and finally on *Trübsal*.) The contrapuntal feat must be seen to be believed.

But this piece impales the believers in absolute music on the exceptionally sharp horns of a dilemma. Their belief may be stated in the words of Dr. Hugo Leichtentritt:* "Bach, like Handel, makes a great distinction between his vocal and his instrumental music. The vocal music is full of picturesque symbolic touches, while the instrumental music relies almost exclusively on purely musical constructive features. It does not try to describe anything; it has no titles, no poetic programs. *The Well-Tempered Clavichord, The Art of Fugue*, the organ preludes and fugues, the suites, the Brandenburg concertos are not program music in any sense of the term, but *music as absolute as has ever been conceived.*" (This is not one of the Brandenburg concertos, but is as absolute as any of those.)

The slow movement, then, when the music was purely instrumental, had no reference to extramusical experience, and we wronged the composer by reading into it even that sense of somber profundity which we attributed to it. For somberness and profundity are adjectival, not substantive, concepts. But the basic passacaglia-theme, in the light of our elements, is a substantive portrayal. (See Ex. 28, opposite.)

Surely these are the tensions and the consequent imaginal motor impulses of a spirit in travail? The biblical text, with extraordinary appro-

* *Music, History, and Ideas*, (Harvard University Press, 1948), p. 148. (Final italics mine.)

priateness, objectified the substantive sense already resident in the music; but it did no more. For both the sense of tribulation and (at the sudden firmness of the cadence) something of the assurance which, with the words, became a promise that the kingdom might be entered, were in the music from the beginning. Once more, the music defined the words — unmistakably (if more generally) in the instrumental version; more amply in the choral elaboration; but the sense is fundamentally the same.

Ex. 28 *

The distinction between "absolute" music and that which delineates the essence of experience is thus arbitrary and meaningless, and the dilemma of the purist unresolvable.

Neither is this conclusion the mere esoteric product of theory and analysis. The distinction between meaningless and meaningful performance is manifest even to the unanalytical but percipient ear. The meaning of music itself — and the meaning communicated by imaginative performance — is an implication of experience in which the hearer can share, to the extent of his own experience, his musical sensitivity, and his imaginative power. Meaningful music may thus prove meaningless to the unimaginative, or to the imaginatively unawakened; but, as the performance of our Bach concerto revealed, it is unwise to underestimate the imaginative powers of the unlearned. They may, as Mr. Kirkpatrick did (see the quotation, p. 89), objectify the implied experience in terms of some imagined factual condition or event. That is a natural endeavor, for experience originates in encounter with objective fact, and is mostly understood in terms thereof. But such imagery is at best only illustrative — the substitution of a single, possibly doubtful aspect of the experience for

* Observe, at A, the laborious rise to D, the alarming drop to Eb, and the ensuing silence; at B, the more uncertain climb (on the diminished triad) to Eb with its succession of lesser ascents and further downward slips — the last another major 7th to Bb; at C, the more positive ascent, in the lower phrase of the figure, to a precarious (because out-of-key) stability on Eb; at D, the most groping ascent and the most catastrophic drop of all, to Ab; and at E, with sudden firmness and assurance, the attainment of a stable foot-hold.

the whole, and the consequent reduction of the dimension of the experience to the dimension of its fraction.

This hazard we also ran in our verbal estimates of the expressive value of our illustrative examples. Our purpose, however, was to show that these values existed, rather than to present our findings as full and complete accounts of musical meaning.

To the extent to which these values exist, sound criticism must take account of them. To assume that they do not exist is thus not merely to evade a difficult problem. It is to vitiate at its very outset the critical effort. Our discrimination of the elements of musical expression thus seems to us to offer a fairly dependable means whereby judgment of the elusive but indubitably existent values of expression may be added to that critical apparatus which the structural analysis of music has already provided.

XI

The Past and the Future of the Elements

W E H A V E thus far attempted to answer, relatively to a period during which a generally undisputed technique of musical composition was practiced, the question: *Can* music express emotion rooted in extramusical experience? Considerable importance for our argument must also attach to the question: *Has* music, in periods prior to that we have considered, expressed emotion? For our elements, observed as functioning within the musical substance, must have evolved along with that substance; the evolution of music did not begin with the period we have illustrated; and earlier structures, gradually assuming the forms we have observed, may also show a gradual approach to the expressive purposes we have defined.

THE ELEMENTS IN THE PAST

The substance of music, as far back as it can be historically traced, has always been compounded out of the two structural elements we still find in it — tone and rhythm. Rhythm, in primitive music, not only stimulates images of motion in its hearers. It *represents* motion (which is a manifestation of energy), and thus impersonates not only human but superhuman powers — the forces of nature and the Great Spirit which directs them. Tone, whether produced by voices or instruments, has the same function — to such a degree that timbre, for its own sake, is of little moment. Organization, consequently, seems to the uninitiated hardly to exist. This is a mistaken impression; but primitive forms are so far dictated by an expressive purpose that they can be grasped only by one who understands that purpose. Yet rhythms and tone-stresses, however different from our own, already represent tensions and motor impulses characteristic of that feeling which worldly experience evokes.

Tone and rhythm had similar meaning for the Greeks, who contrived the earliest civilized music of which we have any detailed knowledge.

Their art, however, differed from our own almost as much as does primitive music. Their fundamental scale was very like our own; but it admitted smaller intervals than are compatible with our notions of harmony, and its tones were related, quite differently, to a different tone-center. Also, music was so intimately bound up with poetry that it constituted, both aesthetically and expressively, an adjunct of language. Its rhythm was almost completely dictated by the quantitative verse to which it was set. The direction of its melodic line was for some centuries similarly adjusted to those pitch-inflections which (quite without dynamic stress) constituted their speech-accent. (These came to be marked by the three accent-signs, acute, grave, and circumflex, which indicated the direction of the inflection.) Concord and discord were recognized, but as existing between successive, not simultaneous, tones. Harmony, as we hear it, was thus unknown.*

Partly, no doubt, through its intimate relation to words, but also through its intrinsic appeal as an art of tone, music was recognized by the Greeks as a significantly expressive art. Even ethical values, which all modern musical theory repudiates, seem clearly to have attached to their Modes. There emerged also a purely instrumental art, enormously popular, chiefly for lyre and aulos. Plato condemned it (apparently since it lacked explanatory words), but Aristotle (*Problems*, XIX, 29) says that "melodies, which are mere sounds, resemble dispositions." Just how that resemblance was effected by the composer or was recognized by the hearer is quite unknown; but that this music bore recognizable relation to extramusical experience seems certain. That some elemental functioning of the musical substance for expression existed is a justifiable conclusion; but to search for those elements in a substance so obscurely understood would be indeed a fantastic adventure.

In Christian belief and its attendant culture, music found new purposes and new freedoms. The almost wholly propitiatory attitude of pagan worship and sacrifice was abandoned for the joyous adoration of a Father by the children He loved; and this belief, however it might become theologized by the learned, effected for the underprivileged especially a new bond of union. The spontaneity of its joy was reflected, before a fixed liturgy was established, in a large literature of hymns, lyrical both in sentiment and in utterance.

* It *was* speculatively imagined, as a consonance of fifths or fourths — see the *Problems*, attributed to Aristotle, XIX, 18.

The Past and the Future of the Elements

Both in Greek and Latin, these poems abandoned the quantitative versification of the classic tongues, substituting an "irrational" quantity which is hardly distinguishable from the accentual versification of English. A vital rhythmic ictus thus appeared; for speech-accent and rhythmic stress coincided throughout, as they had been forbidden to do in quantitative verse. Melody, adapted to such verse, found a new and vital freedom and at the same time a simplicity and directness of syntactical pattern appropriate to the ears and voices of whole congregations.

The popularity of the hymns was great. To the severer theological minds it was also suspect.* For as the Church grew in numbers and wealth through the accession of wealthy and educated patricians, its ritual became correspondingly organized; and ritual and spontaneity are not compatible. The texts of the ritual were in prose — often more exalted in thought than the hymns, but demanding, in those portions appointed to be sung, quite another mode of utterance than that of the hymn.

The product is a type of song now known as Gregorian chant. It was gradually elaborated to a degree that made it quite unsuited to congregational singing, so that trained choirs, in the Mass, "impersonated" the congregation. The artistry of this chant is above praise. Its appropriateness, however, is to the text and the thought of the ritual — both of which, for the simple worshipper, were more remote than the immediate and personal joy of the hymn — so that it was gazed at with admiration, rather than comprehended, by the generality.

The Chant, for many devoted students, expresses even more fully than the polyphony of the 16th-century masters the exaltation of the religious consciousness. Like that consciousness, however, the essence of it hardly bears analysis. The description of a Gregorian Mode, merely as a tone-series, is easy; the definition of its musical meaning, all but impossible. Its tone-stresses relate to a modal "Final," far less compelling in tonal gravitation than our tonic. Its rhythm is disputed. Elements of expression corresponding to those we have described are thus probably not determinable.

Under the cloak of conformity to ritualistic propriety, but in response to pressures also tainted with extraliturgical interest, the most fertile of expressive resources — harmony — was invented. Slowly and by indirection came chromatic alterations of melodic interval (*musica ficta*), de-

---

* St. Ambrose at Milan was accused of bewitching the minds of his people through his hymns.

stroying the purity of the Modes, but gaining at last the far-reaching cohesions of tonality. Upon the principal of tonality, indeed, depends that adjustment of the intrinsic motions and tensions of the musical substance which yields what we have called the elements of expression.

A succession of musical forms results. Each of these, in the period of its currency, is lovingly perfected. But the attainment of perfection does not insure permanency. The taste whose persistence made possible that perfection also changes — capriciously, in part, but more essentially because wider than artistic interests have changed. The sonata, judged by purely musical standards, is in no sense a more highly perfected form than the fugue which it superseded in popular favor; neither was the opera a more perfect form than the madrigal. In every case, the later form followed the earlier, not because of any property of growth discernible in the organic structure of music, but in response to extramusical ideas for whose expression a new form, whatever might be its purely musical perfection, was a necessity. Along with the human creatures it interprets, music evolves. *But there is no intrinsic evolutionary force in abstract artistic forms.*

THE ELEMENTS IN THE FUTURE

The foregoing will suggest that throughout its history music has been understood and practiced as an expressive art. Its structures have been designed for expressive purposes as well as for their value of form; and the elements of expression have emerged within successive forms in response to the pressure exerted on creative minds by those images of experience which, in their emotional aspect, music could portray.

Those pressures, in the 20th century, have been strong. Conventions of belief and behavior, under the illumination which science has thrown on both animate and inanimate matter, have altered profoundly. Musical forms, which reflect conventions of belief and behavior, have altered correspondingly. The alterations, however, appear as a more drastic contradiction of former conventions than is recognizable (in the myopic view of those immediately involved) in the changing current of life. Art moves, in new directions, faster than its public. But it would be silly to suppose that the 19th-century conventions of musical utterance could suffice for the 20th. We have tried to show that the elements of expression evolved, through a kind of mutation, in the successive periods of growth of the musical organism. It is pertinent to our problem to inquire whether, or how far, in the striking mutations evident in contemporary musical structure, the basis — and perhaps the fact — of expression has also changed.

In the 'twenties, the proponents of the new doctrines put forth claims as to the purposes and achievements of the new structures which were both perplexing in themselves and considerably contradictory of each other. With an assurance perhaps more portentous for aesthetics than for the art itself, we were warned that no older principle of musical structure would survive in the glorious new day that was dawning. Even when the language of the new theory was decorous and its apparent method academic, the implication was as rubicund as the most violent revolutionary could desire. Down with the diatonic scale (the revolutionists said) and with the tonic that gave it sense! Down with effete chord-structures in superposed thirds! Down with themes — those trite texts upon which older composers built their tedious musical sermons! Down with sequences, with naked rhythmic symmetries, with the banalities of repetitive structure that went by the name of form! Down with romanticism and its sticky softening of formal contours! Down with the Wagnerian leading-motive and its base, non-musical associations with mere external fact! Down with the symphonic poem — that subtle degradation of musical purity that out-motives the leading-motive in turning music into narrative! Down, even, with the conscious, critical act of composition! No longer shall composers create music; music must create itself in the composer.* For science, almost wreaking destruction upon the imagination of man through its logical insistence that every effect must have its physical cause, has nevertheless hit upon the one saving discovery that may redeem the imagination from oblivion — the discovery of the subconscious.

Not in man's objective bodily self, nor in those superficial indices of behavior-impulse (words and their inflection; bodily attitudes and gestures; the glance of the eye; the contour of the lip) that have long been supposed to reveal character; not even in his pondered, tested judgments of reality and significance in social or physical or psychological phenomena; but in that amazing Atlantis of the spirit, the subconscious, long submerged but at last brought to the surface of life — here at last is the one indubitable reality: the source of knowledge at once true and tran-

---

* A plausible parallel thesis — that criticism makes itself in the critic — does not seem to have been consciously propounded. No supernal power of inference, however, is needed to deduce it from the diatribes just rehearsed.

169

scendental. Here, we were to believe, was revealed the true province of art — the exploration (apparently impossible to objective science, the real discoverer of the subconscious) of those hidden springs of motive and conduct of which all conscious thought and all considered action were henceforth to be seen as the distorted surface.

Pah! The subconscious, thus viewed, is merely the refuge of fools. It is evident, in the first place, that the subconscious existed — and operated, just as it does now — long before it was "discovered." Also, it requires no unusual penetration to see that the conscious utterance of a strictly subconscious impulse is impossible. For to become conscious of a subconscious impulse — to lift it out of the region of subconsciousness and find utterance for it in the conventional procedures of language or art, is to mingle it with conscious awareness and so to destroy irrevocably its identification as subconscious. Granted that the artist, in creative moments, attains to something like clairvoyance: that he becomes aware of impulses, sensibilities, perceptions to which ordinary men are blind — is that *attainment* attributable to the subconscious, which is itself incapable of perception? Granted that he cannot tell, when his work is done, just how it was done: can hardly believe that he, as he ordinarily knows himself, could have done it — does that prove that his conscious structural effort, or for that matter his obscurer creative effort, was made by and in the subconscious? Such unpremeditated art is indeed possible only to skylarks.

On the other hand, to express that which once was in part subconscious but which now, by the might of genius, is brought within the ken of consciousness and interpreted intelligibly to it, is neither new nor revolutionary. The most precious part of genius — that which does *not* consist in the capacity for taking infinite pains — has always been recognized as the capacity for sensing, behind obvious externals of thought and action, the reality of human impulse. Art objectifies life not only as the living know it, but as they feel it. It is therefore our highest intimation of reality; for life itself — to consciousness, our only critic of reality — is the most indubitable of realities.

Just as those strange exudations arising out of the subconscious contribute incalculably to our conscious awareness of reality (our experience), science has contributed, by discovering what might figuratively be called the subconscious of the atom, hitherto unsuspected energies. Whether or not these and similar elemental revelations in animate matter suggest a new interpretation of the human organism, it is apparent that many smug conventions of human behavior which ruled before the 20th century are undergoing, in the light of those discoveries, a pretty thorough revision. The relatively narrow field of behavior represented by art is no exception. The avowed aim of the revolutionary proposals recited a moment ago was the emancipation of music from the trammels of older convention, and particularly from the smug tyranny of the tonic. An eminent 19th-century French literary critic once remarked that emancipations, for the most part, turned out to be no more than changes of servitude.* How far that pregnant remark may apply to our musical revolution is a question pertinent to our whole inquiry.

The revolution — or rather, the civil war between the musicians — is over. Many emancipations have been achieved. The musical idiom of the 20th century differs as unmistakably from that of the 19th as that of the 19th differed from the idiom of the 18th. Reconstruction is still in progress, revealing objectives and reconciliations hardly envisaged by the instigators of the revolution. Among these is the objective of expression. How far its process and its possible attainment have been altered in the establishment of the new idiom is a problem we cannot ignore. To explore it we must examine the new techniques and, by comparing them with the old, attempt to evaluate the emancipations achieved.

The actual music of the revolutionists struck the unaccustomed ear as violently as their proposals struck the mind. The new techniques were difficult, both for the composer to master and for the hearer to grasp. The new problems of structure naturally absorbed the attention of the composers. Consequently the value of expression was for some time either ignored or (what is nearly the same thing) considered as identical with the value of form. Hanslick's views, long derided and apparently abandoned, were rescued from oblivion and took on new life. The new structures would have horrified that anti-Wagnerian; but in the new musical perspective they could still be recognized as *tönend bewegte Formen*. In that perspective the new endeavor — to expand the now intolerably narrow boundaries of musical syntax — appears wholly commendable.

We outlined, in Chapter IV, the structural principles — all finally dependent on the recognition of the tonic — which were now to be com-

* Emile Faguet, *Seizième siècle*, Boivin, Paris, new ed., n.d. (*"Avant-propos,"* p. 1). He is speaking of the emancipation from Scholasticism achieved by the Renaissance.

bated. We may briefly summarize them here as they appeared to their ene-mies. According to classical theory, every note in a musical sentence which did not show a theoretical relation to every other note was wrong. (Wrongness usually struck the ear as discordance.) But even the untrained listener could see that notes which sounded right in Wagner or Strauss would have sounded wrong in Mozart or Palestrina. He would also see that these "right" wrong notes (actually, discords) made the musical sen-tences into which they were introduced more periodic — more suspense-ful and exciting. Perceiving no more than this, the layman would be dis-cerning the essence of that evolution which, for the modernists, was reaching a dead end with the end of the 19th century.*

An awareness of tonic-gravitation as expanding underlay all the ap-proach to this dead end. But it could easily be shown that this commonly accepted tonic-awareness was not an essential, but was really only a con-vention, of musical thought. Both the Greek and the Gregorian Modes had been based on other (and weaker) tone-centers; and the tonic had demonstrably been established by the influence of harmony. In turn, it had intensified the cohesions of harmony. Equal temperament had vastly increased the number of available permutations and combinations of the twelve notes of the scale, but their availability was still governed by the influence of the tonic. That number was not infinite. Whether or not it had been exhausted by, say, 1910, the end was in sight.

The troublesome limitations being manifestly due to the governance of the tonic, it appeared that one way — and perhaps the only way — to establish a new principle of tone-relation was to cut the Gordian knot — to abolish the tonic. Explicitly by the Schoenberg school in Germany, and implicitly (for the average hearer) by leaders of other groups, the tonic was repeatedly led out to execution. But (to borrow a delightful Hibernianism from Ernest Newman) it turned out that the stroke which cut the Gordian knot killed the goose that laid the golden eggs. For, as Schoenberg presently acknowledged, the resultant atonality so far weak-ened the cohesions upon which musical structure depended that to create

* If the horizon of that same hearer were extended so as to embrace the 13th and 14th centuries, he would also see that the "arbitrary" discord (unprepared and unresolved, and hence non-syntactical) of that period was an evil from which music became emancipated through the discovery of a workable process of preparation and resolution. This emancipation through restriction is as significant, theoretically, as Monteverdi's later championship of unprepared discord. But it is much less stim-ulating to the progressive mind.

large musical designs, such as the symphony, was no longer possible. The demise of the tyrant, however, was gleefully celebrated in the 'twenties. Yet we shall see (if we may be allowed to extend our debt to Erin) that the tonal goose turned out to be Hydra-headed.

For the strict theorem of atonality turned out to be indefensible. Schoenberg himself abandoned the term for "pan-tonality"; his greatest disciple, Alban Berg, vigorously repudiated the theorem itself.* Ernest Krenek, also, in expounding the twelve-tone system, taught that tensions implied in a given tonal complex must be respected in the ensuing progression. And Josef Rufer, himself a Schoenberg pupil, quotes (in his *Composition with Twelve Notes* etc., London, 1954) a large number of composers who pursue the dodecachordal system in individual ways.

No pursuer, then, of the atonal will-o'-the-wisp has ever caught that elusive prey. We have designedly allowed some mention of the twelve-tone movement to precede our brief discussion of that system in order to show, in advance, that that same awareness of tonal gravitation upon which so much of the functioning of our elements of expression depends is still a factor in contemporary musical thought. The restrictions of 19th-century tonality have been largely relaxed, both by the twelve-tonalists and by composers who dissent from their views. No discussion of the many varied procedures of contemporary composition is possible in our space; but since the average ear is unable to distinguish the technical basis of any "modern" composition, the present state and the future of our elements may at least be somewhat illuminated if the twelve-tone technique is examined, chiefly in its aspect as a possible vehicle of expression.

In bare outline, the twelve-tone system is as follows:

The twelve tones of our familiar octave scale are to be understood as capable of progression from one to the other in entire freedom from the gravitational influence of the tonic. From these notes, so understood, a "tone-row" or "basic shape" is constructed, normally (but not necessarily) comprising all twelve of the notes. Once established, this row becomes the structural basis (only faintly analogous to a "main theme") of the composition. Its notes are, in part, so selected that they do *not* convey (or betray) any impression of tonic-governance. Once begun, the row (or in later developments, the chosen fragment of the row) must be continued to the end; but the notes may appear either consecutively (as melody) or

---

* See his talk on atonality in N. Slonimsky, *Music Since 1900*, Coleman-Ross, 1949.

simultaneously (as harmony), and any note may be taken in any octave. In developments, the row may be transposed to any degree of the scale; it may be inverted; it may be played backwards; and this retrograde form may also be inverted. Rhythm, in contrast to this meticulous prescription of tonal succession and combination, is regulated only by the composer's ingenuity.

The student of classical counterpoint, confronted by the rigors of that technique, at first feels himself reduced to a state of galling servitude. The prescriptions of dodecaphony, by comparison, suggest a reduction to slavery. Yet Schoenberg averred that, having mastered the system (which he denied inventing, since it seemed to him pre-existent), he was able to compose in it with all the freedom of youth. Composers of very different background have found it similarly fertile, even when its method is relaxed or only partially employed. Imposing musical structures have indubitably been erected on this plan.

The hearer who approaches such structures only with the expectancy of finding the familiar cohesions of tonality is naturally bewildered. Only repeated exposure to the new stimulus can remove these expectations, which are really prejudices. Such exposure, however, will prove that — to put the matter quite simply — you can understand this music if you try to.

Or at least you can understand its structure. Its principles of cohesion — without which no larger principle of structure can be erected — are indeed unfamiliar, and are nowhere indicated in that theorem of atonality which assumes absolute freedom of progression for every note. But that theorem, as seems to have been generally admitted, will not hold. Whether the essential gravitational tensions, indicative of tonal progression, are still wholly intuited by twelve-tone composers, or can ultimately be reduced to "laws" similar to those governing tonal structures, is no matter. They exist.

How greatly they differ from tonal tensions can be quite clearly indicated. The twelve-tone octave contains twelve tones and no more. The tonal octave, on the other hand, *may* exhibit thirty-six. This difference is apparent in the fact that, in the inversion of a row, a given interval — e.g., the diminished *fourth*, B♯ up to E — may properly appear as a major *third* — E down to C.* In tonal music the peculiar tension of the dimin-

* An ingenious system of notation for twelve-tone music, based on this tonal identity of enharmonic notes, has been proposed by Warren Wirtz. The position of the triangular note-head to the right or the left of its stem indicates whether it is natural or flat, and the line or space on which it stands completes the identification

ished fourth — highly significant for the expressive value of the first theme in our C♯-minor Bach fugue — and of many similarly alterable intervals, is unmistakably noted. In twelve-tone music it is lost. No tone in the conventional chromatic scale has a single, fixed *note-name*. What is usually called C may be B♯ or D♭♭ in other contexts, and every other tone may similarly have three different names and three different meanings. The "spelling" of music has never been fully regularized, but the tensions inherent in tonal progressions, however they are spelt, exist, and often, in proper notation, are highly significant.

Nor are these tensions, in tonal music, merely melodic. We have seen how subtly an accompanying harmonic tension may affect the expressive meaning of a melodic note. In twelve-tone music an analogous loss to that which we noted in melody must occur. How far it is compensated for in the harmonic structure of the twelve-tone system it is impossible to say. Twelve-tone harmonies will normally be produced by sounding simultaneously the notes of a segment of the row. The harmony of a given composition is thus considerably pre-determined by its tone-row, *and is to that extent peculiar to that composition*. It appears possible, indeed, that the distinctive character of twelve-tone compositions (sometimes clearly perceived even by the uninitiated) is rooted in this, as it were, spontaneously invented harmony.

Just as in any older music, there are here — and in the contemporary music of other than twelve-tone composers — fluctuant tensions. They are less precisely measurable than in older music; but what might be called a norm of tension can be fairly clearly perceived in any contemporary work, and the fluctuance around this norm can be sensed by almost any hearer. Tensions contribute significantly to the concept of design. The new tensions may also be observed by an imaginative listener as similar to the nervous tensions characteristic of emotional experience — in a word, as expressive.

In the minds of those who undertook to solve the portentous new problems posed by the atonal manner, the structural rather than the expressive value of dissonance-texture was naturally uppermost. As the history of music abundantly illustrates, a new musical structure, even when erected out of familiar materials, may appear, in the perspective of existing convention, difficult to comprehend. A new structure erected out of

wholly without the tangle of sharps and flats which, in the conventional notation of twelve-note music, becomes extremely confusing to the eye.

unfamiliar materials is vastly more difficult. The very substance of the new structures is so unfamiliar to the uninitiated as to appear new. It is not so. It is the same old substance of tone and rhythm, even though it evokes in the unaccustomed listener the incredulous question, "Do you call this music?"

Our concern is here not with the perplexities which this listener must resolve for himself, but with the values which, when his perplexities are resolved, he may find there. He found the old music expressive in a way which our elements in some measure account for. By comparison, the new music appears unexpressive. Our concern is thus with the questions, What, in the new music, has become of the elements of expression? Do they still exist there? Are they actually or only potentially operative — and in either case, how far?

The answers are probably implicit in our examination of the new music, but they may perhaps be brought into sharper focus. The element of ideal motion, at least in so far as it may be equated with rhythm, is essentially unchanged. New rhythms have of course been contrived, awakening new images of motion. But to be expressive an image of motion must appear as more than an abstract pattern of movement. It must appear as the image of a motor impulse, sensed by the listener as suggestive of enactment by his own actual or imaginal motor equipment.

It can hardly be doubted that, in its necessary preoccupation with problems of structure, earlier 20th-century music contrived for the most part what now appear as abstract motion patterns. How far these may prove to have been potentially expressive, and how far the composers of the present period of reconstruction may succeed in relating new rhythms to new actualities of motor impulse — these are questions of the future.

The *fact* of tonal tension exists even more patently in the new music than in the old. Its derivative, the *element* of tone-stress, is not correspondingly evident.

The earlier 20th-century composer, preoccupied with the problem of deporting the tonic from the musical realm, dealt with tonal tensions chiefly as contributions to the atonal structure which alone could effect that end. In this endeavor, he established a norm of tension so high as to be sensuously repellent to the average listener. The gentler tensions of that listener's familiar music had yielded not only the sensuous pleasure which had from the first attracted his interest, but also those intimations of emotional character which made him regard music as the universal language. The new tensions, viewed in that same perspective of expression, seemed to him highly unrealistic. This music did *not*, in Professor Pratt's phrase, "sound the way an emotion feels." It merely evoked unpleasant emotion out of unpleasant sensation.

In the more detailed perspective of our expressive elements the same objection holds. The actual value of an expressive utterance will not, of course, strike home to every hearer at first contact. Only the more obvious communications — which ordinarily have a correspondingly shallow content — can be thus immediately apprehended. But while for the few the extreme tensions of dodecaphony *may* possess an esoteric expressive suggestion extraneous to purely musical interest, there is little evidence, either in the music itself or in those treatises which expound the system, that other than syntactical value is to be considered by the composer.

This conclusion, however, must be acknowledged to represent the not unprejudiced view of the author. The treatises on dodecaphony deal with the structural problems, not with the aesthetics, of that system; and they quite properly stick to their subject. Our problem is that of musical expression; our immediate concern is the persistence of the elements of expression; and we chose to discuss the twelve-tone system because, while it appears to us more indifferent to expression than any other, its rhythms and its novel tensions, guided by an image of experience and thus directed toward the purpose of expression, may well show that even here those elements persist.

That persistence — which indeed evidences no more than the persistence of a conscious endeavor to relate music to the general experience of men — is more apparent in other contemporary styles. Such almost classic modernists as Bartók, Honegger, Milhaud, Prokofieff, Vaughan Williams, and even Stravinsky (in spite of his vigorous denial of expressive purpose not only in his own work but in music itself) frankly pursue — and achieve — expressive aims which seem to us clarified when the stresses and rhythms of their music are observed as the tensions and motor impulses of feeling. The more excogitated manner of Hindemith, based on his own expanded view of tonality, is the vehicle of an avowed expressive purpose so positive that even its moral implications are acknowledged.*

* For a not too technical exposition of his method, see Chap. 5 of his *A Composer's World*, entitled "The Means of Production." For his views on implied moral values, ibid., Chap. 4, "Musical Inspiration," *passim* and especially p. 64f. (Harvard University Press, 1952.)

The emancipation achieved by "modernism" thus appears, in the light of our elements, as indeed no more than a change of servitude. It is the overseers — the inventors of new systems — who have changed, and not the actual master, whom every inventor of a system will still gladly serve. For that master is still dimly visible as the imaginative spirit in men, attempting to explore and communicate the realities of experience as they are felt.

EPILOGUE

❧ XII ❧

Music as Metaphor

No t only in the swiftness and vividness of its expressive suggestion, but in a certain aspect of its whole expressive process, music largely resembles metaphor. Indeed, to set forth this analogy in detail will in some measure summarize our whole thesis, and perhaps present it in a desirably succinct form. That effort may thus occupy us in our final chapter.

The analogy is indeed somewhat remote. To set it forth will require a good deal of apparent circumlocution. Thus our final reasons, which must rehearse in another perspective much of what has gone before, may appear to the reader as two grains of wheat in two bushels of chaff. Yet, since the chaff-choked reader is under no compulsion to follow, we shall pursue our analogy to the end. For it seems to us to illuminate clearly the process and the achievement of the effort at musical expression.

We must begin with a discussion of the verbal figure.

We use language so spontaneously for the utterance of those peculiar mental impulses which we call thoughts that the words we utter seem to us the primary substance, and our sentences the pattern, of thought itself. Many, indeed, have held that we think, and must think, only in words.

This cannot be true. For words are patently the symbols of something; that something is the mental image of experience which it is the purpose of language to communicate; and that prior image, according to its clarity and according to the store of verbal symbols we have accumulated, initiates and dictates our verbal utterance. Without that image, words would be no more than an incoherent outcry.

Experience is imaged, primarily, in terms of things and acts, of their qualities, and of the relations between them. Thus our "parts of speech" — nouns, verbs, etc. — are distinguished as such accordingly as they symbolize these "parts of experience." But our images of experience are far more vivid than are the bald definitional meanings of the words which denote the things of which our experience is primarily composed. More exactly, then, we should say that words are really the symbols, not for things as they are outside ourselves, but rather for our awareness — our mental image — of these things.

This awareness is almost always fluctuant in vividness. Hence the meanings of words are not fixed and stable. Instead, they grow and diminish accordingly as the object symbolized is great or little in the immediate perspective of consciousness. Incessantly, indeed, the user of language will strive to give to his words that precise shade of meaning which, while indicating the factual identity of the things and acts essential to his image of experience, will also reveal their immediate aspect and value as he *now* sees them.

Language exhibits a high ingenuity in the adjustment of its substance to this subtle purpose. It keeps a generally unchanged form (pronunciation) for those verbal symbols which denote the parts of experience involved in the idea to be expressed; through syntactical structure it arranges and modifies these symbols appropriately to their significance in the total image of experience; and beyond all this it finds a way of giving new and flexible contours to the conventional pronunciations of words — contours which, as we may say, cause them to smile or frown accordingly as their immediate emotional value changes. These contours are inflections — "bendings" — which add a significant meaning-increment to the definitional and syntactical sense of words.

Another type of meaning-increment may be added by bending the sense itself of words in what we call figures of speech. Metaphor is the most vivid of these figures since it adds the greatest and the swiftest increment to the definitional sense of words. It does this by asserting an identity — remote, unsuspected, often almost wholly unreal (but on that very account more illuminating) — between two objects of experience. In this "equation," one of the objects is illuminated; the other is the illuminator. (In the metaphor, The wages of sin is death, sin is illuminated in the light of its fearsome earnings.)

The value of the figure, however, lies less in the equation itself than in the illumination it throws. Indeed, the real purpose of metaphor may be achieved almost without emphasis on the identity of two unlike things, but, as I. A. Richards notes, through "some common attitude which we may (often through accidental and extraneous reasons) take up towards them both." * Very often, indeed, a peculiar inflection is essential for the conveyance of metaphoric meanings. Indeed, in some cases where the strict form of the figure (the "equation") is not even suggested, inflection alone may achieve the illumination which is the essential end of metaphor. The verbal symbol for a single object, that is, may be so far "self-illuminated" by inflection that that object, while still visible in its unfigured guise, assumes a new identity and thus, through inflection alone, fulfills the real function of metaphor. Examples are not hard to find.

The word water symbolizes an object whose value — which is to say, whose emotional interest — for me differs greatly in different circumstances. Signifying the mere substance, imbued at the moment with no particular interest, my utterance of the word will be inflectionally inert. Signifying my attitude toward it as a drink offered in place of something more stimulating, my inflection (now equivalent to "Ugh!") may "transfer," in the literal sense of the word metaphor, that symbol for a mere substance into the image of an object of repulsion and so of repulsion itself. And, to leap at once over a long gradient of imaginable instances to the opposite extreme of feeling, we may note how men have delighted for more than two thousand years to imagine the inflection of that famous shout of Xenophon's soldiers — "Thalassa! Thalassa!"

To call this shout — this mere inflection of a word — a metaphor may well offend the rhetorician's pride in his science. Yet it did signify a transfer. The water acclaimed by those soldiers (even though their word for it was now "sea") was for them the water of life; and in the swiftness and vividness of this suggestion the shouted word fulfilled the function, if not the precise form, of metaphor. The name of a single object, self-illuminated by no more than its exuberant inflection, became the symbol for an object so different in value as to appear, for that moment, another object.

At any rate, through this inflection (a mere phenomenon of capriciously fluctuant pitch) that symbol acquired a powerful increment of verbal and emotional meaning. Substantively, the word still signified an object which, in its ordinary aspect, would have been mentioned with indifference. Inflection alone gave it its now extraordinary import.

* See the last two chapters of his *Philosophy of Rhetoric* (Oxford University Press, 1936). He has just been analyzing the metaphoric sense of "duck" when used as implying "tender and amused regard." Here, inflection is the principal agent in conveying metaphoric sense; for the blunt inflection applicable to this word when it symbolizes a web-footed fowl would hardly flatter the damsel to whom the phrase "You *are* a duck" was addressed as an expression of tender and amused regard.

Being a phenomenon of pitch and loudness, that inflection bore a certain resemblance to music. In the absence of any precise gradations, whether of pitch or rhythm, that resemblance was indeed faint. Yet, through a tiny fraction of music's capacity for precise pitch-inflection — while of course retaining the bare definitional sense of "sea" — that symbol achieved a metaphoric illumination of experience. It is rational to inquire more specifically into this capacity of music.

The verbal inflection remained, in function, adjectival. It "modified" a word whose primary significance was substantive in nature. Yet the meaning that word acquired was no longer adjectival. The sea, in another than its ordinary context, now became quite another object. Inflection, that is, all but achieved the function of definition. It did so, not by "equating" the sea with another dissimilar, illuminating object, but by illuminating the sea itself in the light of the emotion felt by those who saw it as (in our feeble phrase) the water of life. And it thus all but fulfilled the function of metaphor.

In immediacy and vividness this illumination would be hard to equal. Even the most compact of verbal metaphors, fulfilling the prescribed pattern of an asserted identity between two unidentical objects, would appear, by comparison, halting and colorless. Nor did this shout, while fulfilling the function of metaphor, wholly fail to fulfill that prescription. There was indeed but one *object* involved — the sea; but its *aspect*, as illuminated by that shout, was new, and the comparison strictly demanded by the figure was now not that between two disparate objects, but between two disparate aspects of the same object.

Inflection sufficed to establish that comparison. The physical aspect of the sea as a body of water was all but obliterated, but its new aspect — significant beyond any verbal definition — was identified in a term no more elaborate than the electrified shout of its bare objective name. For here was an experience whose emotional import involved more associations than there was either time or vocabulary to define. What other vehicle than an outcry — a bending of the voice to the high exigency of the moment — could have sufficed?

But music is also, and primarily, a bending of the "voice" — an inflection — possibly adjustable to the utterance of even more complex exigencies of feeling. With its wide tonal range and its complexity of texture it is certainly capable of more subtle adjustment, to a greater variety of purposes, than is verbal inflection. Its components, tonal motion and tension, do indeed function primarily toward the creation of a tangible musical body — a musical form. The hearer, perceiving this object and assimilating its sense, undergoes what may properly be called the musical experience itself. The musical organism, functioning thus, may be indefinitely expanded and refined; but so long as it is seen in this aspect of a tonal structure, no intensification of its tensions and motions will effect or even initiate that transfer upon which metaphor depends.

Tension and motion, however, are characteristic of human as well as of musical bodies. In the musical body, they function *for* structure. In the human body they function *through* its pre-existent structure as the translation into activity of impulses aroused in that body by what may be succinctly designated as experience. Indeed, our response to physical and mental encounters of every sort is "enacted" through motions and tensions which, interpreted, appear to correspond with remarkable fidelity to our total awareness of the circumstances (largely external) out of which they originate. But the body of music — physically no more than a substance of tone and rhythm — may be so constructed as to manifest, in its tensions and motions, compulsions beyond those which function for structure — compulsions which so far resemble the drives which actuate the human body that the musical body *becomes* human — becomes Buffon's *l'homme même*. Is not this metaphor? Is there not here a palpable transfer of the behavior-patterns of the body of tone into the behavior-patterns of the human body — even of those which enact the farthest reaches of its consciousness?

Our elements of expression were, and could have been, identified only as the agents of such a transfer. In fact, when trying to identify them, we called the primary step in the "evolution" of the elements a transfer of tension and motion from their status as functioning *agents* (not elements) of formal structure to a status as *elements* (not agents) in a design still structurally intact but in purpose now essentially representative. The "thing" which motion and tension can portray will naturally be a thing of which motion and tension are themselves characteristic. Such a thing is the human nervous system under the stress of emotion. But that system is far more than a mechanism for neuro-motor response to a stimulus. It can not only register in the memory its tensions and motions as bodily states. It can also relate these states to their apparent causes. In a word, when its stress is produced by the impact of the world upon it, that infinitely complex mechanism is acquiring experience.

185

The purport of experience as it impinges on the nervous system is ordinarily assessed in a manner called intellectual. The external facts contributory to experience are registered, more or less accurately, in the memory, and are further organized into a composite awareness which, in various degrees of literalness, forms what we have called an image of experience. But the purport of that image is not perceived merely through observation of those contributory items of fact. They have, indeed, as external events, no meaning in themselves. They merely occur. The only meaning they possess is their significance, immediate or remote, for him who encounters those facts. That significance is his valuation of the experience.

He makes it, to be sure, at his own peril. He learns painfully to assess significance in terms of his own needs, and to reassess it when the ineluctable needs of that society of which he is a member are forced upon his attention. This image of experience and this valuation of it form his idea both of the world and of himself as having being in that world. And that idea cannot but be tinged with emotion. For emotion, in the constitution of his being, preceded the intellection which, evaluating the world of experience, taught him also to control his emotion; and it still remains, after control has been learned (as far as it can be learned) as the mainspring of that action through which the welfare — or the ruin — of being is achieved.

Indeed, our ultimate understanding of our fellows and ourselves, although we describe it in apparently objective terms of kinetic or potential action, is primarily conceived in terms of emotion. For emotion, mingled in consciousness with the intellection which directs it, becomes motive, which stands to conduct as simple sensation-stimulus stands to motor reaction. Our final assessment of conduct may thus be made largely in terms of motive. For while motive may appear as no more than the index of ill-considered action, it may also appear as the visible index of pondered experience. So seen, it may also be interpreted as "character" which, literally, is "engraving," and which appears, whether in the face or in more general patterns of behavior, as having been chiseled there by the sharp tools of experience.

The hall-mark of a significant art-work, as of a significant person, is this readily apprehensible yet vastly comprehensive manifestation of character. In art-works, as in men, it is understandable only in the light of that type of experience which it distills. Since all art, in our view, is an

186

abstraction, this is true of "abstract" art as well as representative (in which category we have considered music). The rectangle may hold, for the painter, depths of experience which it does not possess for the geometer; and none may gainsay (however few may perceive) the truth of that artist's perception. Music, as abstract design — which, however representative of non-musical feeling, it must also be — plumbs similar depths. But if — as we contend, and the world at large appears to hold — the area of experience bounded by the rectangle or the tonal design is narrow in proportion to the area which that world must somehow interpret, the gain in depth will continue to be weighed against the loss in experiential perspective — for the most part to the disadvantage of abstraction.

All the arts, after their fashion, serve the purpose of communication — essentially, the purpose of language. All, indeed, strive for and often reach the vividness of metaphor, the most vivid of linguistic devices for communication. Music, originating in the region of consciousness where the meaning of experience is felt, has an almost unique aptness for metaphoric utterance.

The immediate trend, in all the arts, appears to be away from "pure" abstraction toward a new manner of representation. What addition the now established "vocabulary" of abstract musical thought may make to the scope of musical representation is a question for the future to answer. But the world will not gladly renounce the communicative power of that wonderful tongue which, in the shortest life-span of all the arts, has contrived so metaphorically to reveal the spiritual stature of men.

APPENDIX AND INDEX

Appendix

F E W systematic attempts to account for the generally recognized fact of expressiveness in music have appeared. Daniel Gregory Mason, in the first and last chapters of his *From Grieg to Brahms* (Macmillan, 1902) championed, rather amusingly, the then current notion of music as a "presentative" art. A. Sorentin assembled a small but somewhat impressive body of instances in which expression patently occurred, but his system, whether in selecting or analyzing his examples, was wholly empirical. Albert Schweitzer, in his notable study of Bach, confidently ascribed definite expressive value to various "motives," clearly analogous to the Wagnerian leading-motives; but he made no attempt to account for their expressive value on any basic principle. Aaron Copland's *Music and Imagination* (Harvard University Press, 1952) recognizes clearly but does not attempt to explore the problem. Several recent studies, which seem for the first time to acknowledge that if expression occurs it must rest upon some principle, have been noted in the text.

An exhaustive study of the problem has, however, just appeared — *The Language of Music*, by Deryck Cooke (Oxford University Press, 1959) which not only recognizes the significance of musical expression but attempts systematically to account for it. Since his idea of the elemental forces differs considerably from our own, some comment on this book is imperatively called for.

Chapter 2, entitled "The Elements of Musical Expression," begins thus: "The task facing us is to discover exactly how music functions *as a language*, to establish *the terms of its vocabulary*, and to explain how these terms may legitimately be said to express the emotions they appear to." (Italics mine.) He thus embarks, quite knowingly, on the perilous adventure of equating musical with linguistic utterance — a procedure aesthetics has always viewed with alarm.

He continues (p. 35): "Beginning with the basic material — notes of definite pitch — we must agree with Hindemith that musical works are built out of the *tensions* between such notes. These tensions can be set up in three dimensions — *pitch*, *time*, and *volume*; and the setting up of

191

such tensions, and the colouring of them by the *characterizing agents* of *tone-colour* and *texture*, constitute the whole apparatus of musical expression." (Italics Cooke's.)

This, generally in accord with the distinctions underlying our elements and accessories of expression, seems undebatable. But his account of the properties of the tensions is harder to grasp: "Pitch-tensions can be regarded in two different ways — as *tonal tensions* (what the actual notes of the scale are) and as *intervallic tensions* (in what direction and at what distance the notes are from one another)." For conventional theory describes the functions (which Mr. Cooke calls tensions) of the seven *diatonic* notes of the scale in the terms, tonic, supertonic, mediant, etc., as explained in the footnote on page 43; but Mr. Cooke amplifies this description by assigning a specific tension to each of the twelve notes of the *chromatic* scale, and these are his "tonal tensions."

To establish these he offers a rationalization of the scale — a curious identification of its "actual notes" — as derived from the harmonic series of upper partials. For in his scale the chromatic notes, except for the augmented fourth (F♯ in the C-scale), are *flatted* notes only. His tonal tensions thus arise only between major and minor intervals, except for the augmented fourth and the diminished fifth; and these two, which are audibly equivalent, he hardly distinguishes from each other. The other augmented and diminished intervals, whose peculiarities are highly significant for purely musical as well as for expressive meaning, are wholly absent from his catalogue of "tonal tensions."

The danger of regarding music "as language" — as a medium of communication based upon an all-but-symbolic "vocabulary"—does not terrify Mr. Cooke, who with high assurance assigns to each of the tensions he recognizes a considerably positive verbal equivalent. He summarizes these ascribed values thus (p. 89f.): Minor second: spiritless anguish; Major second: pleasurable longing (but as passing-note, neutral); Minor third: stoic acceptance, tragedy; Major third: concord, natural third [in the harmonic series]: joy. (We need not complete the catalogue, which will prove to be the foundation of his "vocabulary of musical terms.") He adduces, in all, hundreds of examples of the use of melodic intervals, by composers from the 15th to the 20th century, for the utterance of specific characteristics of feeling. These characteristics (which in most cases are indicated also by the texts to which his examples are set) are largely in accord with the catalogue of primary values assigned to the tonal tensions summarized above.

Curiously, the "intervallic" tensions, which he presents in far less than their actual number, are subjected to no such precise analysis. Had they been, the resulting "vocabulary" would have been alarmingly extended. Yet the omission is perplexing, since these tensions may so modify the supposedly intrinsic character of the tonal tensions as to obliterate their primary expressive suggestion.

Like the intervallic tensions, those of time (roughly equivalent to rhythm) and of volume (which he appears to regard as also elemental) are here given, by comparison with the tonal tensions, no more than passing mention. They are invoked, however, in ensuing discussions, as occasion demands. One is forced to the conclusion that tonal tensions are to be regarded as collectively forming the primary, and all but the sole, *element* of musical expression. Upon this general basis he proceeds, in the next chapter, to identify and verbally define "Some Basic Terms of Musical Vocabulary."

These "terms," still largely viewed as the product of tonal tensions, turn out to be highly familiar melodic progressions, as, for example, 1–3–5 (as C–E–G in the key of C); as 5–3–1; or as "arched" 5–3–(2)–1, where 5 ascends to 3, and 2 intervenes before the descent to 1. These "terms" are observed as highly distinct in expressive value accordingly as they appear in major or minor.* In the complete "vocabulary," the major and minor thirds and sixths appear as by far the most determinative of the tonal tensions. Verbal definition of the terms, similar to those offered for the tonal tensions, are suggested. Mr. Cooke is quite aware of the inadequacy of these words for the full conveyance of the expressive sense contained in the music; he realizes also the contribution to that sense made by the "time-tension" (rhythm) and by the stresses of intervallic tension (harmony); but he seems unaware that his verbal definitions, insistently presented as valid indices if not as fixed equivalents of the musical meaning of the "terms," may assume for him who accepts them a significance quite unsubstantiated.

For Mr. Cooke's elements of expression by no means exhibit all the intrinsic force needed to bear the burden of meaning he imposes on them, nor is that burden (too precisely defined in terms of tonal tension only) clearly referable to the source from which he derives it. What he offers, indeed, appear not as *elements* but simply as *instances* of expression — plausible enough in most cases, but scarcely reducible to any principle of

---

* Mr. Cooke defines the sequence 1–3–5 thus: "To deploy the major triad as a melodic ascent . . . is to express an outgoing, active, assertive emotion of joy" (p. 115). Contrariwise, the descent on 5–(4)–3–(2)–1 expresses "incoming" emotion, and "will convey a sense of experiencing joy passively, i.e., accepting or welcoming blessings, relief, consolation, reassurance, or fulfilment" (p. 130).

This ascription of character is somewhat over-confident. The *Parsifal* Prelude begins with the unharmonized melodic sequence 1–3–5 (Ab–C–Eb). Granted that the association with the Eucharist remains to be established, will any hearer find in that phrase an outgoing, active, assertive expression of joy? But again, is there a more outgoing, assertive, jubilant phrase in all music than that which Beethoven contrives on the "passive" sequence 5–3–2–1 (and completes with the whole supposedly "relaxed" *downward* octave of the major scale) in the Finale of the A-major Symphony (at bar 3 of the second ending of the second section of the first theme)?

expression implied in his primary assumptions. He seems to have glimpsed, in his indicated tensions of pitch and time, the elemental significance of what we have called tone-stress and ideal motion; but in his over-sharp definition and verbalization of a part only of the whole energy contributory to expression he has blurred the image of experience which, to become really expressive, they must evoke.

His over-elaborated distinction between tonal and intervallic tensions seems to us sharply evident in his analysis of the opening motive in *Tristan* (p. 188f.). He arbitrarily takes the first three ('cello) notes, A–F–E, as in the key of D minor (the "arched" 5–3–2 which with 1 is one of the "terms" of his vocabulary, defined on p. 138 as denoting a "flow and ebb of grief"). The final 1 (D♯ when the "Tristan chord" enters) is called E♭ (the 'hopeless' minor second), perplexingly equated with D♯. But "this note is harmonized as though it were a new tonic minor, [again E♭] by the melancholy secondary seventh chord on its supertonic (F), a chord which derives its gloom from the presense of the anguished minor sixth."

But this assumption of D minor as the initial key, and of a modulation to E♭ minor, is quite gratuitous. Many a hearer has doubtless taken the first notes as the "arched" 3–1–7 in F major — equally wrongly. For the notation, the *Tristan* chord, and the whole behavior of the motive clearly imply nothing else than the key of A minor. The initial note A, then, is tonic; The F is thus (in our definition) intrinsically an active note (not the "sad" third of the minor mode); its activity ("anguished," if you like, since it is the active minor sixth) is intensified in force through five slow, unmarked rhythmic beats; and this energy takes it, with hardly a hint of rest, right over the normal rest-tone, E, to D♯ (*not* E♭!) — the augmented fourth of the key, far more active than was the F.

But now, to produce Mr. Cooke's supertonic seventh-chord, Wagner's B must become C♭, and G♯ must become A♭. "So far," Cooke says, "so intensely sad." But by a kind of prestidigitation quite unsuggested by Wagner's wholly rational notation, this chord becomes "a complex of tensions on the sharp side of A" (*major!*): "the F in the bass is the anguished minor sixth of that key; the G♯ is the 'violently longing' major seventh of A itself; and the B is the dominant of the dominant, having a stiffening, binding effect."

Wagner's notation, on the contrary, seems to us perfectly lucid. The key is A minor throughout; the D♯ is the augmented sixth above the submediant, F, already long held by the 'celli in precisely that sense, but now transferred to the bass; the B is the augmented fourth above that same F; the G♯ (whose rising implication is unmistakable from the beginning, so that its enharmonic, A♭, is in no sense suggested) is a sort of rising appoggiatura to A; and when this A appears (on "six" as did the 'cello E) we have the familiar "French Sixth." (6+ 4+ 3) above the submediant of the minor key, where it most frequently occurs. The audible equivalence of the Tristan chord to the supertonic seventh (for the average ear, one of the most appealing of discords) is an extraordinary achievement in musical semantics, for (as Mr. Cooke appears to recognize) it veils the intrinsic harshness of the involved augmented intervals in enharmonic ambiguity. But it also overfloods the sense of anguish with a tang of irresistible allurement. Through the upward tendency of the chromatic melody line, it resolves by way of A♯ into the relative quiet of the simple dominant seventh, which itself resolves only into silence. But that silence is now filled with the meaning of that simple harmony (bulged as was the word strange in our illustrative stanza by its extraordinary context) — a meaning which Mr. Cooke's sophisticated interpretation of its component intervals can in no way account for. This music is not a portrayal of chemically compounded emotions. It is a metaphor of experience.

Index

THE following is an attempt to locate for the reader various topics, details of the argument, or other references not indicated in the table of contents. Since most of our discussion is in the form of argument, revolving around a relatively small array of fact, indicative reference in the usual shape of catch-words has been extremely difficult to provide; for those words, in the context of the argument, have a considerably wider significance than they possess when isolated. For the same reason, there has been no attempt to list every occurrence of any given term throughout the book. The index should serve, however, to link together the essential features of the argument which, of necessity, have been presented piecemeal.